FABERGÉ: IMPERIAL CRAFTSMAN AND HIS WORLD
exhibition album

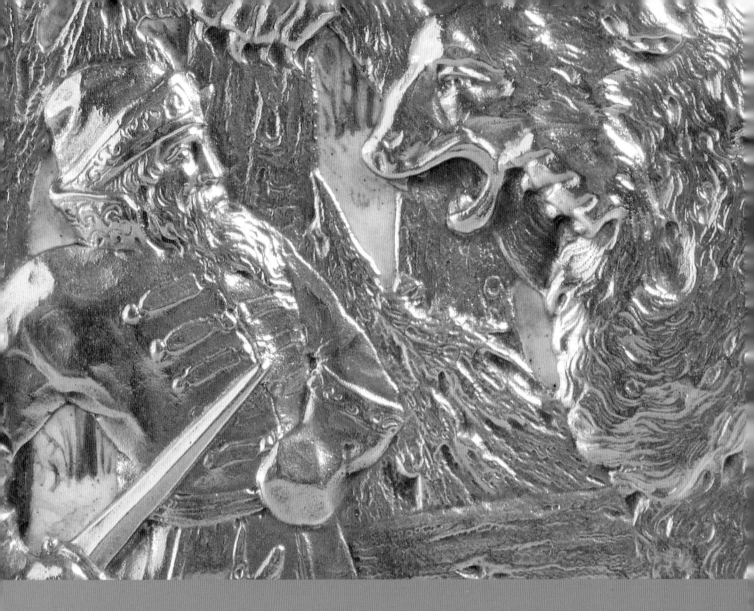

'TAKING INTO CONSIDERATION …
THE NEEDS OF THE HIGHER CLASSES
OF SOCIETY … WE PROVIDE … THE
LUXURY AND EXPENSIVE GOODS TO
SATISFY THE MOST REFINED TASTE …'

Peter Carl Fabergé

'JEWELRY: …IT REPRESENTED, NO DOUBT, A STUPENDOUS OUTLAY OF MONEY, BUT IN THOSE DAYS WE JUDGED THE JEWELRY BY THE BEAUTY OF ITS DESIGN AND COLORS, NOT BY ITS VALUE.'

Grand Duke Alexander Mikhailovich

'FABERGÉ IS THE GREATEST GENIUS OF OUR TIME, I ALSO TOLD HIM: VOUS ÊTES UN GÉNIE INCOMPARABLE.'

Dowager Empress Maria Feodorovna

FABERGÉ
IMPERIAL CRAFTSMAN AND HIS WORLD
EXHIBITION ALBUM

Robert Steven Bianchi
Director of Academic and Curatorial Affairs, Broughton International, Inc.

Booth–Clibborn Editions

First published in 2000 by
Booth-Clibborn Editions
12 Percy Street
London W1T 1DW
United Kingdom
www.booth-clibborn-editions.co.uk

© Robert Steven Bianchi 2000
© Broughton International, Inc. 2000
© A La Vieille Russie, Inc. 2000
© The State Hermitage Museum, St. Petersburg 2000
© The State Museums of the Moscow Kremlin 2000
© The Forbes Magazine Collection, New York 2000

Edited by Mark Sutcliffe
Designed by Christopher Wilson

ISBN 1 86154 204 6

Printed and bound in Hong Kong

CONTENTS

Preface

In keeping with our past practice, suggested by our visitors, we at Broughton International have produced this Exhibition album in which we have discussed the life and career of Peter Carl Fabergé and reproduced in full the texts of the gallery panels, each accompanied by a selection of works of art described by extended captions. The dimension given is that of an article's height, unless stated otherwise.

An exhibition of this scope – the largest ever mounted about Fabergé – has been a monumental task filled with the myriad details associated with major, international loan exhibitions. It has been a pleasure, therefore, to have been able to work with a group of dedicated individuals who labored long hours on short deadlines in good humor. I wish, therefore, to take this time to thank Jack Stefany and Emilio Pittarelli of Architectural Consultants. Rolanda Norton and Mark Sutcliffe at Booth-Clibborn Editions, and Deborah Bull and her staff at PhotoSearch responded with alacrity and accuracy to my requests for textual and photographic assistance, respectively.

I would be remiss if I did not also acknowledge my indebtedness to Dr. Géza von Habsburg . Although our approaches to the exhibition and our interpretations of the man and his oeuvre were not always congruent, he steadfastly and ungrudgingly shared with me his knowledge about 'Faberganiana'. For that I express my gratitude.

The opening of this exhibition is personally bitter-sweet. All that I have learned about the jeweler's art I have been taught by my uncle, a master in his own right, and all of those lessons learned in his Manhattan workshop over the years have been brought to bear on my work on this exhibition. I deeply lament his passing, shortly before the opening, and dedicate this album to his memory as a small token of my large indebtedness.

Dr. Robert Steven Bianchi,
Director of Academic and Curatorial Affairs
Broughton International, Inc.

PETER CARL FABERGÉ
(18 May 1846 – 24 September 1920)

**1. Peter Carl Fabergé
sorting loose gems**

His family tree

The history of the Fabergé family begins and ends in exile. Peter Carl's ancestors were Huguenots, French Protestants, living in Picardy in the north of France. In 1685 King Louis XIV revoked the terms of the Treaty of Nantes. That revocation fostered religious persecutions resulting in a mass exodus of Huguenots from France, the ancestors of Fabergé among them. The severity of this persecution was such that his fleeing ancestors were compelled to conceal their French Huguenot roots by changing their name. These ancestors first settled in Schwedt-an-der-Oder, not far from Berlin, now the capital of Germany.

About a century later, around 1800, Peter Fabergé, a carpenter by trade and the paternal grandfather of Peter Carl, moved his family to Pernau in Livonia, on the Baltic Sea, because Catherine the Great, Tsarina of Russia, had instituted an enlightened policy of religious toleration. Realizing that the stigma attached to his French Huguenot roots had now been removed, Peter reverted to a form of his family's original name and became a willing subject of the tsarina as a 'naturalized' Russian. At this stage in the family history, fact appears to have been blended with fiction because there is a tradition (albeit unsubstantiated) which records that a certain goldsmith from Würtemberg, Germany, named either Farberger or Farbiger, traveled to Russia on commissions for Catherine the Great, and that Peter Carl Fabergé of St. Petersburg was his direct descendant.

His father

Peter Fabergé and his wife, Marie-Louise Elsner, had only one child, Gustav Fabergé (1814-1893), who was born at Pernau in what is now Estonia. As a young man, Gustav traveled to St. Petersburg, where he apprenticed with a master jeweler.

2. Gustav and Charlotte (née Jungstedt) Fabergé in Dresden, Germany, about 1850

In 1842, Gustav Fabergé married Charlotte Jungstedt, daughter of a Danish painter, and in that same year opened his own shop in St. Petersburg at 12 Bolshaya Morskaya Street. The couple had a son who was born on 30 May 1846. Peter Carl's only sibling was his younger brother, Agathon (1862-1895), who eventually joined the family's firm but died suddenly at the age of 35. In time, Peter Carl attended the Gymnasium Svetaya Anna (St. Ann's School), a rigidly run, German-language private school, one of the best and most fashionable in St. Petersburg. His attendance at this institution points to his father's advantaged economic position.

In 1860, Gustav Fabergé retired and moved to Dresden, Germany, but still retained ownership of his firm. Peter Carl traveled to Frankfurt-am-Main, Germany, in order to apprentice, and enrolled in the local trade school in Dresden where his studies could be monitored under the watchful eye of his father. He undertook study trips to England, and traveled to Italy where he studied the work of Florentine enamelers and goldsmiths. The objects which Fabergé saw in museums during his training abroad, and the styles on which he worked as an apprentice, were to characterize much of his own production. As significant as these European influences were on Peter Carl Fabergé, those from France were equally important for him because of the prevailing influence of French culture on tsarist Russia of the period.

3. Agathon Fabergé

In 1870, having returned to St. Petersburg a few years earlier, the 24-year-old Peter Carl took over the management of his father's firm. Shortly thereafter, in 1872, he married Augusta Julia Jakobs. Although not a raving beauty, Augusta was nevertheless considered a good match because she came from an artisan's family, her father having served as an overseer of the imperial furniture workshops under the reign of Nicholas II's grandfather, Alexander II.

4. Augusta Julia (née Jakobs) Fabergé

A suggested character sketch of Fabergé

Fabergé's personality and character remain elusive, but a few random recollections help to provide a character sketch of this extraordinary entrepreneur in broad stokes. Apparently very set in his ways, Peter Carl Fabergé was adamant about those things which he hated, and writing letters topped that list. He was laconic in speech, and always came to the point as quickly as possible, with the result that he detested those who talked unnecessarily. He assiduously avoided politics as a subject of any conversation. He had little patience with legal documents, disliked studying bank accounts and sales sheets, and harbored a disdain for those who would join organizations of individuals banded together for the protection of some special interest or group.

He could be witty. He once told a fawning client, upon returning to his gallery in quest of square Easter eggs which she had mistakenly thought he would be creating, that he was simply not up to such a complex task. He could enjoy a practical joke.

Peter Carl hated to travel and often did so without packing. On one occasion he was almost prevented from checking into a fashionable hotel in Nice on the French Riviera because he had no accompanying luggage. In the end he was recognized for who he was, and the reservation was honored. He then shopped for the needed toiletries and clothing.

5. Fire-screen Frame
varicolored gold, enamel, and pearls, marks: FABERGE, initials of Henrik Wigström, 1908–17. The FORBES Magazine Collection, New York.
This double sided picture frame is ingeniously designed as a fire screen surmounted by a floral wreath and four sprays of laurel. Elaborate swags of flowers and garlands decorate the rectangular panels within which are portraits in pearl-bordered oval apertures of Tsar Nicholas II on one side and Tsarina Alexandra on the other.

Defining the nature of Fabergé the craftsman

The appeal of collecting works by the House of Fabergé was, and continues to be, twofold. On the one hand, there is the snob appeal, inspired by the exclusivity of these beautifully crafted objects. On the other hand, owning an object by the House of Fabergé provides a tangible link with the last resplendent monarchy of Europe, a monarchy overthrown by a revolution of cataclysmic proportions. In many respects, Peter Carl Fabergé made Tsar Nicholas II and his wife, Tsarina Alexandra, famous – or, rather, posthumously famous. Their names have become so identified with Fabergé's oeuvre and the name of his firm that the words 'Fabergé', 'Nicholas', and 'Alexandra' have become, in the minds of many, inextricably linked.

Peter Carl Fabergé has been called the greatest of craftsmen in the age of craftsmen. Peter Carl was a stickler in this regard and always held the artisans in his employ to the highest standards of technical accomplishment. His sophisticated technical innovations must be

understood in terms of the changes being brought about by the Industrial Revolution. That Revolution introduced new technologies and new materials which Peter Carl began to exploit to the fullest. Understanding the potential for interchangeable parts, Fabergé could design a complex commission in such a way that a bowl might be sculpted in hardstone off-site by one of his craftsmen and perfectly fit into a mount created elsewhere by another craftsman. He developed a rainbow of enamel colors and perfected their application onto both gold and silver. He was also cognizant of the array of new consumer products spawned by the Industrial Revolution which the world had not consumed before. Toward the end of the 19th century, portraiture was revolutionized by photography. These photographs required picture frames, and the House of Fabergé excelled in their manufacture. His production was prodigious because of the importance ascribed to framed photographs of loved ones within homes.

Electricity introduced the light bulb, which in turn required electrical lamps with shades. Peter Carl's contemporary, Louis Comfort Tiffany, created lamps which relied on the extensive use of glass so necessary for the casting of light from those bulbs.

8. Cylindrical Bellpush enameled silver-gilt, signed with the Imperial Warrant mark of Fabergé, 1896–1908. Michael and Ella Kofman Collection. The design features a six pointed star chased with acanthus leaves, a cabochon moonstone push piece in its center, and elegantly decorated with chased laurel swags on the sides. The impetus for such articles was the result of the ever more common use of electricity brought about by the Industrial Revolution. These electrical bells were used not only for doors to announce visitors but also for rooms replacing handbells or other devices used to summon domestics. In order to meet the demand for this new consumer product-line, Fabergé's output of electric bell pushes was tremendously large.

9. Square Desk Clock gem-set, enameled gold-mounted bowenite, signed Fabergé with initials of Michael Perchin, before 1899. Private Collection. Clocks became more commonplace as time began to dominate social intercourse. Everyone admits that the hands and dials of Fabergé's clocks are extremely easy to read, and this characteristic is in keeping with Peter Carl's insistence on consummately crafted products. This example is artfully adorned with two sprays of lilies-of-the-valley applied to the hardstone bowenite face. The buds are made of pearls and the chased yellow gold leaves are tied with a diamond and ruby-set ribbon.

Electricity was also harnessed for electrical bells, not only for doors to announce visitors but also for rooms replacing handbells or other devices used to summon domestics. As a result, Fabergé's production of electric bell pushes was tremendously large. Clocks became more commonplace as time began to dominate social intercourse. It is widely acknowledged that the hands and dials of Fabergé's clocks are extremely easy to read, and this characteristic is in keeping with Peter Carl's insistence on consummately crafted products. To this list can be added the countless cigarette cases, umbrella handles, opera glasses, desk sets, ash trays, stick match holder-strikers and the like which the firm also created.

What is the appeal of Fabergé?

There is another component to Fabergé's oeuvre, namely, his *objets de fantaisie*, trifles of the imagination, perhaps, which seem to serve no useful purpose other than to delight and entertain. The major objective of these, as in all of Fabergé's creations, it would appear, is an unconcealed desire to transmit a feeling of good will evident in even the most modest pieces. Every one of his objects was planned not to impress by its magnificence or cost but with the uncomplicated aim of giving pleasure to the recipient. The objects, therefore, were never intended to be imprisoned behind the plate glass of museum exhibition cases. Rather, each Fabergé object was meant to be savored and to be shared with and enjoyed by others. Indeed the appeal of Fabergé may have been unwittingly best summed up by the Soviets for whom these works of art were anathema. In an attempt to denigrate both Fabergé and his oeuvre, they denounced his creations as playthings of the rich, which of course is exactly what

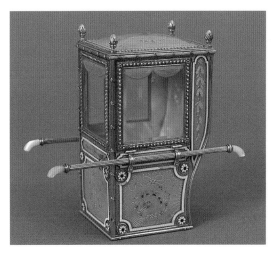

10. Sedan Chair of Louis XVI
Design enameled gold, mother-of-pearl, and rock crystal,
inscribed Fabergé with initials of
Michael Perchin, 1899–1908.
Private Collection, Courtesy Ulla
Tillander-Godenhielm.
Connoisseurs often remark that
the world of Fabergé is a world in
miniature, dominated by objects
of fantasy whose entire purpose is
to please. This delightful example
is a case in point. Its two carrying-poles, the terminals of which are
whimsically designed as
artichokes, are removable. Its four
panels are decorated with motifs
symbolizing love, the arts, and
gardening. The rock-crystal
windows are meticulously
engraved with simulated curtains
and reveal the cab's mother-of-pearl appointed interior.

11. Vase-shaped Pendant gold
and enamel mounted nephrite
with the initials of Michael
Perchin, before 1899. Private
Collection.
Less than one inch in height, this
pendant features a footed, egg-shaped vase, indebted to amphoras
of ancient Greece. That model has
here been modified because its
attached, curved handles have
been replaced by two angular
ones. Fabergé was fond of the
shape of such ovoid-vases and
ingeniously employed them not
only for jewelry, but also for the
bodies of clocks and other articles.

those Fabergé confections were and still are, and the very reason they were designed in the first place.

The pleasure-giving sensation derived from these works of Fabergé may be due in no small part to the Renaissance nature of Fabergé's character. He reveled in humanity and the joy of life, in the delight of living, in loveliness and harmony. By his art he was able to make the fleeting and the ephemeral become eternal.

Fabergé was also a successful businessman and realized the potential financial windfalls that sales of his product lines to less affluent clients could bring. The House of Fabergé continued to serve an elite clientele but offered similar merchandise at prices attractive to what one might call the middle class. Fabergé may have sold only one Imperial Easter Egg a year to Tsar Alexander III, but imagine how many umbrella handles, cigarette cases and picture frames were sold to walk-up customers who desired to own an object from the exclusive House of Fabergé!

In my estimation, the single most important characteristic of Fabergé's oeuvre which contributes to its pleasure-giving sensation is the miniature scale of his works. Fabergé's world is a world of miniatures, and because his works of art are miniature in scale they can be more readily manipulated, that is, easily held in the hands to use or admire. The more readily manipulated an object can be, the more personal it becomes. The more personal it becomes, the more intimate its associations, particularly if the object was presented as a gift. That enhanced intimacy contributes to the enjoyment of viewing or handling the object. For these reasons, Fabergé's best work is found in those objects created on a small scale.

Just what, exactly, did Fabergé do?

Mentioning the name of Fabergé today, an image generally forms in the mind's eye of a man stooped over his workbench, visor over his forehead, jeweler's loup over one eye, assiduously creating an exquisite bauble. Nothing could be further from the truth. Peter Carl Fabergé has often been compared to a choreographer, and the comparison is valid. He would coordinate a team of designers who would submit rough sketches for discussion. Sometimes these designs were generated by members of his firm, but on occasion clients submitted their own designs or ideas for commissions. The more expensive a commission, the more varied the materials involved in its creation, the more intense and frequent were these meetings, all chaired by Peter Carl who oversaw every stage of the work. Round-table discussions such as these were a routine part of the firm's quotidian, often staged in Peter Carl's private office where substantive discussions resolved the plan for attack of complex objects. Rumor has it that he would smash to smithereens those objects which either did not meet with his approval or fell short of his high-quality standards.

Fabergé's work force at one time numbered 300 direct employees, with an additional 200 serving as subcontractors. That number included about a dozen carpenters whose sole task was to manufacture the presentation cases for the works of art, as well as a number of independent artisans, who, while owning and operating their own shops, signed contracts and worked exclusively for Fabergé. The majority of his craftsmen were Finns or Swedish-Finns, given the proximity of St. Petersburg to the Gulf of Finland. His direct employees worked exclusively for him under contract in workshops for which he collected no rent. Fabergé also provided his direct employees with all the necessary tools and raw materials free of charge. It seems likely that Fabergé paid his master craftsmen not by an hourly or daily rate, but rather in accordance with the profits earned from the sales of the merchandise they had created. In a perverse way, Fabergé's atelier appears to have been a microcosm anticipating the ideal socialist's economic system which was supposed, in theory, to replace that of tsarist Russia in later communist workers' utopias.

Peter Carl's genius may perhaps be defined as an uncanny ability to recognize what his clients desired and channel the artistry of the legions of craftsmen in his employ and the techniques at their disposal to craft available material into the client's desired work of art. In this capacity, Fabergé acted as a mediator between what was desired and what was technically possible from the point of view of the materials. In this role he revealed his unique talent at conveying his ideas of the design to his craftsmen, and was able to follow that up by coordinating the efforts of specialists, each one expert in the handling of a different material. This delicate balance between the ideal and the achievable, driven by client's needs, may help to explain why his oeuvre is so heterogeneous and why his role in his firm's creative process should be best regarded as one of leading and coordinating. Despite the heterogeneity of his oeuvre, which does not conform to a uniform Fabergé style, the end result is that each of Fabergé's creations is distinctively Fabergé and cannot be readily confused with the creation of another atelier. This distinctive 'Fabergéness' can be attributed to Fabergé's role as a choreographer. A ballet troupe is composed of different personalities often possessed of differing skills. Under the guidance of an experienced choreographer, the troupe gels and performs in a distinctive dance idiom so associated with the choreographer that balletomanes can identify the choreographer and readily distinguish her/his dance style from that of another. In like fashion, Peter Carl had the knack of getting the hundreds of craftsmen in his direct employ on the same wave length, with the result that their communal efforts, under his close, hands-on supervision, resulted in the creation of unmistakably Fabergé objects. That process and its individual results are the real genius of Peter Carl.

Fabergé's choreographic achievements were facilitated by two important characteristics of his work force. First, Peter Carl himself enjoyed a long, professional association with many of his master craftsmen, some of whom he had worked alongside as a young man, when apprenticed to his father's shop. Fabergé himself was probably taught by Hiskias Pendin. Both August Holmström and Erik Kollin, in the employ of his father, continued to distinguish themselves under Peter Carl. Secondly, many of his master craftsmen were personally interrelated. To cite just two cases, August Holmström's daughter, Fanny, married Knut Oscar Pihl, himself a master craftsman for the House of Fabergé. Their daughter, Alma Theresia Pihl, distinguished herself as a designer of at least two of Fabergé's Imperial Easter Eggs. Henrik Wigström, another master craftsman with the House of Fabergé, apprenticed under Michael Perchin, a Fabergé master craftsman himself. Perchin and his wife served as godparents for Wigström's children, and Perchin in his will bequeathed his workshop to Wigström. As such interpersonal relations demonstrate, not only were craft specialties being passed on from one generation to another under the same roof in the House of Fabergé, but Fabergé's own *modus operandi* – the nuts and bolts, if you will, of how his organization functioned – was also being passed down. The value of these family ties exercized in the daily application of what can only be considered hereditary craft skills, coupled with Peter Carl's early hands-on training with some of these very masters, cannot be underestimated. The solid foundation provided by such a unique corporate continuity contributed immeasurably to Fabergé's success as a choreographer.

13. Bowl silver repoussé with the imperial double-headed eagle and Cyrillic inscriptions for 'WAR,' '1914,' and 'K.FABERGÉ,' stamped with Imperial Warrant mark of Fabergé, 1908–1917. John Traina Collection.
Because of extenuating economic circumstances occasioned by World War I, many bowls of this type were created in both copper and brass, so an example such as this in silver was very rare. Its inscriptions are propaganda slogans indicating that Fabergé, like other prominent Russians, was patriotically committed to the war effort. It has been suggested that such articles were given to officers of the Russian armed forces to be used as drinking cups.

Fabergé and World War I

The number of Peter Carl Fabergé's employees swelled to about 500 at the outbreak of World War I, when he was obliged to contribute to the war effort. His workshops began to produce small weapons in keeping, no doubt, with the miniaturist nature of his oeuvre in general, as well as medical supplies. His silver workshops devoted their energies to manufacturing shells and grenades. As the war dragged on, many of his employees were drafted, and his once large work force was now reduced by about 80 percent. Gold and silver were scarce and reserved for the manufacture of military medals and badges. Steel, copper, and brass now became the materials of the hour and Fabergé was quick to exploit their decorative effects.

The Imperial Easter Eggs

Of all of the creations of the House of Fabergé none possesses the mystique attached to the Imperial Easter Eggs. Their centrality to Fabergé's entire oeuvre is so dominant that one immediately thinks of these eggs first whenever the name of Fabergé is mentioned. In order to place these eggs in context, it is worth recalling that the egg was anciently imbued with overtones of resurrection, later a suitable symbol for Easter. The practice of distributing eggs as reminders of Christ's Resurrection began in the Middle Ages, and developed in Russia where the traditional gift of an egg at Easter was accompanied by the recipient receiving three kisses. In Russia, such Easter eggs might be lavishly decorated, as examples of *pysanky*, the art of beautifully dyed Ukrainian Easter eggs, reveal. The practice of presenting actual Easter eggs, therefore, was an established tradition in Russia.

Although received wisdom maintains that the designs for Imperial Easter Eggs were not submitted for approval, and that Fabergé

14. Coronation Egg varicolored gold, platinum, enamel, diamonds, rubies, rock crystal, velvet lining, marks: initials of Henrik Wigström. The FORBES Magazine Collection, New York. Presented by Tsar Nicholas II to Tsarina Alexandra Feodorovna on Easter 1897, the Coronation Egg is one of the most celebrated eggs created by the House of Fabergé for the last two tsarinas of Russia. Commemorating the 1896 coronation of Nicholas and Alexandra, the egg's breathtaking design was inspired by the gold trimmed robes worn by the imperial couple during the coronation ceremony.

At the top of the egg is the crowned monogram of Tsarina Alexandra Feodorovna emblazoned in rose-cut diamonds and rubies, attached by means of a minute hole drilled into the enamel, clearly indicative of the technical skills of its author. The year of the egg's presentation, 1897, appears beneath a smaller portrait diamond at the bottom of the egg.

When the egg is opened, the surprise fitted inside a velvet-lined compartment is a removable replica of the coach in which Alexandra made her grand entry into Moscow at the start of the coronation festivities. Workmaster George Stein labored for fifteen months, sixteen hours a day, in order to complete this gold, enamel, diamond and rock crystal fantasy which is faithful to the original in every detail. A glimpse through the carriage's etched rock crystal windows revealed at one time a final surprise – a tiny egg-shaped emerald and diamond-set pendant which sparkled from within like a gem-set chandelier. The current whereabouts of this jeweled prize is unknown.

It is interesting to note that Fabergé managed to obtain the services of George Stein, who was then earning three roubles a day, by wooing him away from a rival with an increase in pay to five roubles a day and a guarantee of 300 days of work a year. Stein accepted the offer and his annual income soared to 1,500 roubles.

15. Fabergé's St. Petersburg headquarters The flagship office of the House of Fabergé was located in St. Petersburg at 24 Bolshaya Morskaya, opened in 1900. This pink granite, four-story edifice was remodeled by Fabergé, who had been in business for twenty-eight years in collaboration with the architect-designer, Carl Schmidt, for a cost of 416,000 roubles. In keeping with the corporate continuity of the firm, this building was not only a home for Fabergé's family in rooms facing the street with views of the city, but it was also the location of some of his craft studios. So, for example, Hollming occupied space on the first floor; Perchin, then Wigström, on the second; and Holmström on the third. The sales room was also located on the first floor and the establishment maintained a reference library, a feature almost never found in such workplaces at that time. One estimate claims that several hundred individuals worked in the building at any one time.

was given complete freedom in their design and execution, there is evidence to the contrary to suggest that on occasion the Tsar did make suggestions about the theme of a particular egg. We know that Tsar Alexander III was both interested in and involved – either directly or indirectly via His Majesty's Cabinet – in the commission of the Second Hen Egg, which contained as its surprise the sapphire pendant given to the empress in 1886. There is also some evidence to suggest that Nicholas II dictated the juxtaposition of his miniature portrait with that of Peter the Great on the shell of the Romanov Tercentenary Imperial Easter Egg.

In examining the Imperial Easter Eggs as a whole, it is evident that Fabergé took an existing tradition and pushed it to the limit of his firm's collective creative abilities, never once compromising on quality. His Imperial Easter Eggs surpass everything that had been achieved in this genre before his arrival on the scene, and truly represent the very best of his firm's oeuvre. Nevertheless, the firm's ingenuity was taxed, particularly after the coronation of Tsar Nicholas II in 1896 when the commission required the creation of two different Imperial eggs for each Easter season. That ingenuity was further challenged by the demand for similar eggs from other wealthy clients. As a result, the House of Fabergé seized upon the most appropriate of solutions. They created themes for their Imperial Easter Eggs based on the everyday lives and accomplishments of the family of Tsar Nicholas II and Tsarina Alexandra, linking them whenever possible to the continuity of the Romanov dynasty. The results were intimate, personal creations celebrating exceptionally public displays.

The house of Fabergé's St. Petersburg headquarters

The flagship office of the House of Fabergé was located in St. Petersburg at 24 Bolshaya Morskaya, and opened in 1900. This pink granite, four-story edifice was remodeled by Fabergé, who had been in business for twenty-eight years, in collaboration with the architect-designer Carl Schmidt, for a cost of 416,000 roubles. In keeping with the corporate continuity of the firm, the building not only provided a home for Fabergé's family in rooms facing the street with views of the city; it was also the location of some of his craft studios. Furthermore, the sales room was located on the first floor, and the establishment maintained a reference library – a feature almost never found in such workplaces at that time. One estimate claims that several hundred individuals worked in the building at any one time.

Fabergé's presence along Bolshaya Morskaya was very low-key. The building itself was not marked by any large signs. Those in advertising are quick to point out the importance of a doorman, and any one patronizing the fashionable shops along Manhattan's fashionable Fifth Avenue will also recognize the value of such an employee. The doorman at Christie's auction house in New York, Mr. Gil Perez, was recently featured in a profile article in a leading newspaper in which his contribution to the firm's image, and perhaps even success, was documented. The entrepreneurial Fabergé also recognized the value of a good doorman, who was ever-present at 24 Bolshaya Morskaya.

Inside the sales room on the first floor, there was virtually no interior décor. Fabergé's minimalist approach was doubtless intentional so that architectural decorative elements would not compete with his merchandise in capturing his client's attention. Repeat clients soon learned that objects of fantasy were also to be found on the left-hand side of the sales room whereas jewelry was restricted to the right-hand side.

Pricing and profit

There were indeed others who had foreshadowed Fabergé, but once he arrived on the scene, there was only one Fabergé. He established his pre-eminent position by purposefully avoiding the use of large, costly diamonds and other precious stones, and by concentrating on exploiting the potential inherent in more mundane materials. In order to establish market value for his line of production, Fabergé insisted that the value of the craftsmanship which went into the creation of any of his objects had to exceed the value of the materials used. He himself said, 'We are people of commerce rather than artist-jewelers. I have little interest in an expensive object if its price is only in the abundance of diamonds and pearls.' He had his own system of placing a monetary value on that craftsmanship, basing the price of any given object not solely on its material components but on his assessment of its artistic merit. This system accounts for the fact that his firm was such a financial success. Some insight into his pricing schedule can be gleaned from records surviving from his London office. Here, he was meticulous in recording in roubles the exact cost of manufacturing any given object offered for sale in this branch. When one compares that net cost with the retail price, one discovers that Fabergé marked his pieces up 90 to 100 per cent over cost. An excellent self-promoter, Fabergé also informed his clients about his operation: 'The firm's large turnover enables it to sell its wares at very reasonable prices, which are kept as low as is commensurate with maintaining the high quality of the work.' Because he recognized the fact that tastes and fashions change, he also informed his clientele that he would at year's end melt down any items not sold in order to assure the originality of each successive year's offerings. In today's currency, one could find items in his shop ranging in price from a few dollars for a bauble to objects retailing for hundreds of thousands of dollars. He liked to keep in stock at all times a selection which was as varied as possible. This might include smoking paraphernalia, from cigarette cases to match stick holders and ash trays; handles for canes, walking sticks, and umbrellas; fans, opera glasses, combs, snuff bottles, knitting needles, electric push bells, desk accessories such as pen holders, blotting pad holders, stamp dispensers; candle sticks, coffee and tea services, bric-à-brac, garnitures, and full scale pieces of furniture. 'We accept orders for the above-mentioned objects, as well as [orders for] prizes for societies organizing racing and jumping events, and we send out-of-town customers designs, estimates and illustrated price-lists on request.'

He issued catalogues because, he said, 'they live in the provinces, have no opportunity of visiting our premises personally and of seeing for themselves our rich selection of goods.' His catalogue goes on at great lengths to indicate that the articles were sold for the lowest possible price insofar as the meticulous workmanship had to be compensated. He guaranteed to take back or exchange individual pieces provided that these had not been made to order, that they were not damaged, and that they had been purchased fairly recently.

'Taking into consideration both the needs of the higher classes of society as well as the interests of the middle class, we provide both luxury and expensive goods to satisfy the most refined taste as well as inexpensive goods within the reach of the not too well-to-do.' So popular were his dinner service items that people began to speak of 'laying out the Fabergé' rather than of 'laying the table.' The prodigious scope of his oeuvre has prompted one critic to remark, with justification, that the firm of Fabergé was hands-down the largest jewelry firm in the world, ever.

Realizing that the rate of exchange does fluctuate, scholars have nevertheless attempted to calculate the relative prices in current US dollars of the following types of objects offered in Fabergé's sales rooms, assuming that two roubles equaled one American dollar. Miniature Easter eggs and miniature pendants were priced at 5 roubles, or $2.50 each. A standard cigarette case would average 100 roubles, or $50. Clocks and picture frames were comparably priced, each ranging from 200-300 roubles, or $100-150. Animal figurines and flowers were priced in the broad range of between 180-600 roubles, from $90 to $300, but, in general, the flowers were the more expensive, averaging more than ten times the price of an animal. Regardless of what one may think, Fabergé's prices were relatively high. Routinely advertised diamond necklaces were listed at 50,000 roubles, the equivalent of $24,000. He created a Gothic silver table service for Barbara Kelch for the price of 125,000 roubles, or $60,000, in order to replace the one she had initially ordered from Khlebnikov, which she did not like.

In a vacuum, because such prices may be meaningless, the following may help to provide a more complete picture of the relative cost of a Fabergé object in comparison with contemporary prices for other items and services. Dinner at the famous Coubat Restaurant without wine ran to 3 roubles, or $1.50, whereas the best ticket to the famed St. Petersburg Mariinsky ballet would have set one back 25 roubles, or $12.50. In 1885 a general in the Russian army was earning

6,000 roubles per annum; a colonel 4,000. Fabergé himself realized the power of the rouble, and often used it as leverage in order to lure craftsmen away from rival concerns. He managed to obtain the services of George Stein, who was earning three roubles a day, luring him away from Kortman by offering him not only a rise to five roubles a day, but also guaranteeing him 300 days of work a year for an annual income of 1,500 roubles. It took Stein 15 months, one recalls, to craft the miniature coach which was the surprise in the Coronation Imperial Easter Egg.

The Russian Revolution and last years of Fabergé's life

There is a certain irony in the realization that Fabergé's employment package with some of his master craftsmen was strikingly in advance of the system later advocated by the Soviets. He provided them with rent-free spaces in which to work, gave them free of charge the necessary tools and raw materials, and paid his master craftsmen and work masters commissions based on the sales rather than in hourly, or weekly wages. This is not the place to rehash the political events that led to the demise of the Russian monarchy. Suffice it to state here that when the disturbances of 1905 erupted and the streets of St. Petersburg were unsafe because of continued confrontations between protesting workers and peace-keeping Cossacks, Fabergé arranged for his workmen to remain in the safety of their own homes while still continuing to pay their wages.

In a final attempt to save his own firm from becoming a target of the Bolsheviks, Fabergé seized upon the idea of forming a workers' committee, composed of members of his own staff, with the expressed purpose of running the business. This stratagem bought Fabergé some valuable time, but the Bolsheviks eventually nationalized his company in 1918. When they entered his establishment, he asked only to be allowed to put on his hat, and walked out of the door without taking anything else with him, because his habit was to travel, which he loathed, without any luggage whatsoever.

Fabergé then left Russia for good, fleeing to Finland in disguise, with the help of the British embassy. One might speculate on whether this reported assistance was in any way connected with Fabergé's association with the British royal family and the fact that he may still have had significant funds in British accounts, Bainbridge having continued to make sales privately until early January 1917.

When the Russian Revolution reached Latvia on 18 November, Fabergé, now in his seventies, proceeded to Bad-Homberg, Germany, and then on to Wiesbaden, where he was joined by his wife, Augusta, and their son, Eugène. Augusta and Eugène had managed to escape from Russia, and certain death had they elected to remain there, by crossing the border into Finland in late December 1918 on sleigh and on foot through snow-covered woods under the cover of darkness. They then made their way to Lake Geneva in Switzerland, where Fabergé, now 74-years-old, died on 24 September 1920 in Lausanne from what friends and relatives called a broken heart; he often exclaimed near the end, 'This life is no more.' His tombstone of black Swedish porphyry is said to have been inscribed with letters of gold, but Bainbridge maintains that his epithet should have been, 'He was never over-serious.' Augusta Fabergé, his widow, survived her husband by a few years, dying in Cannes in the south of France in 1925.

THE EXHIBITION

Introduction

Peter Carl Fabergé (1846–1920) was born in St. Petersburg, Russia, the eldest son of Gustav and Charlotte (née Jungstedt) Fabergé. After a period of training as a jeweler which included a number of study trips, he returned to St. Petersburg and at the age of 24 assumed full responsibility for his father's firm. Although his life is in many ways a fairy-tale epic of successive, brilliant triumphs, it is also a doleful tragedy which suddenly ended in exile, despair, and death. The Russian Revolution of 1917 toppled tsarist Russia and put an end to all entrepreneurial enterprises. The following year, when the Bolsheviks appropriated his premises, Peter Carl Fabergé merely requested ten minutes to put on his hat and coat. He left Russia as a refugee and eventually settled in Lausanne, Switzerland, where he was wont to remark, 'This life is no more.' He died there, in exile, from what friends described as a broken heart.

Fabergé has been called the greatest craftsman in the age of craftsmen and is known as the owner of the largest jewelry firm ever to have operated anywhere. His name has been linked to a host of extraordinary creations, and rumors still persist that he modified a ruby cup once owned by the legendary Cleopatra. These assessments of the man and his oeuvre are doubtless the source of the almost universally maintained opinion that Fabergé, sitting at his work bench, wearing a visor and using a jeweler's loop, single-handedly created the wonderful works of art on view in this exhibition.

The truth of the matter is surprisingly different. Recent scholarship has established that Peter Carl Fabergé was a master choreographer who orchestrated the production of over 150,000 articles, created in more than a dozen workshops by hundreds of craftsmen working in St. Petersburg, Moscow, Odessa, and Kiev. This exhibition focuses on some of the more important of those craftsmen and places their creations into the broader context of the jeweler's art.

16. Rectangular Picture Frame
silver-mounted nephrite and birch
wood with a wooden back and
strut, initials of Anders
Nevalainen, 1904–1908. Louise
and David Braver.
The workshop of Nevalainen, a
Finn, who began to work under
exclusive contract with Fabergé
soon after 1885, was chiefly
known for its silver-mounted
frames, of which this is an
example. The inner aperture is
bordered in nephrite, or Siberian
jade, one of the favorite
hardstones used by the House
of Fabergé, and applied with
holly leaves and rosettes.

17. Cigarette Case diamond-set
enameled silver-gilt with
diamonds, signed Fabergé with
initials of August Hollming,
1899–1904. John Traina
Collection.
This cigarette case was a 32nd-
birthday present from the dowager
empress Maria Feodorovna to her
son, Tsar Nicholas II. It is lovingly
inscribed, 'To dear Nikky from
Mama, 6th May 1900.' Its gray-
green hue was purposefully
selected because that was the
color of her son's favorite
regiment, the Preobrajensky, of
which he was commander-in-
chief.

**18. Match Holder/Striker in
the Form of a Mushroom**
silver-mounted sandstone on a
gadrooned silver base, the well
lined with silver, with initials of
Anna Ringe, before 1899.
The Woolf Family Collection.
Anna Ringe ran the shop founded
by her husband, Philip Theodor
Ringe, after his death. They
specialized in small articles of gold
and silver created for the House of
Fabergé, such as this match
holder/striker. Naturalistically
modeled with a delightful silver
frog seated to one side, this article
is representative of the more
affordable creations of the House
of Fabergé.

19. Shaped Oval Desk Clock
diamond-set gold mounted
enameled silver-gilt, 5$\frac{1}{8}$ inches,
signed Fabergé, with initials of
Michael Perchin, 1899–1908,
Private Collection.
The design features an applied
gold laurel wreath surrounding
the dial, tied above and below
with diamond-set ribbons. Its base
is chased with acanthus leaves, its
hands are gold, its bezel of seed
pearls. Fabergé relied upon just
two Swiss watchmakers to supply
him with movements. One of
those was Henri Moser of Moser
& Cie, whose signature appears
here. Moser's movements,
uniformly about 1$\frac{3}{4}$ inches in
diameter, generally contain dials
with Arabic numerals and elegant
hands.

**20. Heart-shaped Picture
Frame** gold-mounted and
enameled silver-gilt, 2$\frac{3}{4}$ inches,
signed Fabergé with initials of
Victor Aarne, 1899-1908.
The Woolf Family Collection.
A Finn born the son of a church
sexton, Aarne's speciality were
exquisite miniature frames of
miniature size. The example
features an outer beaded border
applied with four-color gold rose
garlands suspended from a ribbon
cresting.

Sources of inspiration

A selection of works of art created in the 18th century in England, France, Russia, and Saxony evokes the traditions from which the firm established in 1842 by Gustav Fabergé emerged. His chosen field was very competitive, as one directory, published in 1848, reveals with its listing of more than 300 jewelers active in St. Petersburg alone. These individuals were Russian and foreign-born and worked in a variety of artistic idioms.

It should come as no surprise, then, to learn that Gustav Fabergé, having retired to Dresden, Germany, while still retaining the controlling interest in his firm, should summon his son, Peter Carl, to join him in order to begin his training with a view to taking over the family business. That training was supplemented by a number of study trips throughout Western Europe, which included visits to museums and collections in Germany, France, and Italy so that his son might be exposed to a spectrum of artistic styles.

Such training was not in vain because Peter Carl Fabergé was later affectionately described as a 'cultural sponge' – he possessed the remarkable knack of absorbing artistic influences from all periods, past and present, and from many cultures, European to Oriental, and impart what he absorbed to the legion of craftsmen under his supervision. Orchestrating their talents, Fabergé enabled those gifted craftsmen to transform their sources of inspiration into works of art. Whether the artistic models derived from ancient Greece, the Gothic period, the Renaissance, the Rococo, the Neo-Classical period, or even China, the resulting creations were uniquely and unmistakably 'style Fabergé' in character, and immediately recognizable as such. Keenly aware of contemporary trends, Fabergé could direct his ateliers to adopt either the naturalistic forms of Art Nouveau or the geometry and sobriety of Art Déco in order to craft works of art which were never slavish imitations but highly original creations.

21. Figure of an Ostrich and its Keeper jeweled silver-gilt enamel with diamonds, pearls, rubies, emeralds, chrysolite, and agate, 4⅝ inches, created in Dresden, early 18th century. The State Hermitage Museum.
The Dresden masters, particularly J. M. Dinglinger, were famous for such figurines which are characterized by an extensive and varied use of secondary materials. Fabergé surely viewed such works of art during his schooling in that city and was to use them later as sources of inspiration for his own creations.

22. Egg with a Clock on one Side and a *Nécessaire* on the Other varicolored gold with diamonds and enamel, maker's mark now illegible, Paris, 1757–58. The State Hermitage Museum.
According to tradition this clock/*nécessaire* was given to Tsarina Elisabeth I by representatives of the French court as an Easter present. The upper lid, covering the clock, is decorated with a diamond studded monogram of the empress, and bears an inscription in French which translates as: 'Each moment belongs to you.' The lower lid, which covers the *nécessaire* (a small, ornamental case for pencils, tweezers, scissors, etc.) is decorated in turn with the Russian double-headed eagle bearing the coat-of-arms on its chest and the insignia of the Order of St. Peter. This fascinating article was formerly in the collections of the Diamond Room of the Winter Palace in St. Petersburg where Fabergé doubtless had the opportunity of studying it. He was later inspired by the *nécessaire* which served as his model for the outer shell of one of his Imperial Easter Eggs.

23. Perfume Bottle in the Shape of a Peacock gold, silver-mounted diamond-set, 3⅓ inches in length, Russian, mid-18th century. The State Hermitage Museum.
Although there are numerous examples of theriomorphic vessels of 18th century date, this particular object is distinctive because of the extremely high quality of its craftsmanship. The enamel decoration is consummately applied, the mechanism of the lid fastening intricate, and the engraving on the base both delicate and precise.

24. Oval Cameo Box gem-set gold-mounted agate with diamond push piece and rock crystal base, 2⅝ inches in length, initials of maker I.G., Russian, about 1840. Private collection, courtesy A. von Solodkoff.
The principal motif is a time-honored one, namely that of a lion killing a stag, which first appears in the art of ancient Mesopotamia and continues into that of ancient Greece and Rome. In such instances the king of beasts may symbolize the power of a monarch. Furthermore, in keeping with a classification of objects from antiquity, this article is likewise inscribed with an epigraph: 'The cameo surrounded by diamonds was given by Emperor Alexander I to Maria Antonova Naryshkina.' Alexander I is remembered as having defeated Napoleon at the Battle of Borodino in 1912.

2

A national achievement

In order to gauge the originality and unmistakable character that mark Fabergé creations, this gallery presents some of the works of art created by a selected group of 19th-century Russian silversmiths and enamelers. Many of these individuals submitted their works to regularly scheduled exhibitions where expert juries confronted the arduous task of choosing between works of the most famous Russian craftsmen.

In the mid-19th century, Russian silversmiths began to embellish their creations with *champlevé* enameling, a technique whereby the enamel is melted into compartments sunk deeply into the metal. This technique was gradually superseded about two decades later by *cloisonné* enameling in which the deeply sunk compartments are replaced by thin plates applied to the metal's flat surface.

One such craftsman was Feodor Ivanovich Rückert, who, following a practice of the time, was brought to Russia as a lad of 14 by one of the leading Russian aristocratic families, and eventually opened his own, very successful, workshop. This gallery includes a selection of his works of art and others by Pavel Ovchinnikov.

A serf who eventually gained his freedom, Ovchinnikov founded a silversmithing and enameling firm in Russia in about 1850; it grew between the years 1870 and 1917 into the most important of its kind in Russia. On the occasion of the Pan-Russian Exhibition of 1865, Ovchinnikov was singled out for his enamel items, which were regarded as a 'national achievement.' Such was the high level of the competition in Russia which confronted Peter Carl Fabergé shortly after he took over his family's jewelry business.

25. Stirrup Cup in the Shape of a Dog's Head silver, 2⅞ inches in length, with initials of workmaster P.K., c. 1870. The State Hermitage Museum. In the middle of the 19th century Russian silversmiths in St. Petersburg introduced cups and wine goblets fashioned in the shapes of heads of animals and birds. They were well received and became immensely popular. This article is typical of that production and is distinguished by the finely chased details of the dog's fur. The House of Fabergé was later to build upon this tradition when the silversmiths of its Moscow branch created an array of silver articles incorporating into their designs any number of animals.

26. Throne-shaped Saltcellar silver, signed with Imperial Warrant mark of Pavel Feodorovich Sazikov, 1861. The State Hermitage Museum. Engraved with the monogram NA, this saltcellar was presented to Tsarevich Nicholas Alexandrovich during a tour of his realm. Chased to imitate wood-grain, this article is decorated with a figure of a peasant woman offering a loaf of bread. The saltcellar and that image are references to the Russian ceremony of *khleb i sol*, or bread and salt. As a sign of hospitality, whenever a tsar or tsarina visited a town or city in their realm, the merchants and landed gentry would present them with a loaf of bread on a round dish covered with an embroidered towel. The salt would either be placed within a hole hollowed out in the loaf or contained in a separate cellar.

27. Monumental Circular Presentation Charger gem-set silver-gilt and enamel with a ruby and emeralds, 24²₃ inches in diameter, signed with the Imperial Warrant mark of Pavel Ovchinnikov, 1882. The Khalili Family Trust.

The border contains 13 roundels, each of the 12 smaller ones adorned with the coat-of-arms of a different Russian city, the larger thirteenth depicting St. George Slaying the Dragon, emblematic of Moscow. The center contains an heraldic double-headed eagle, the symbol of the Romanov dynasty, its center applied with a ruby surrounded by emeralds. The accompanying inscription reads: 'On the day of the holy coronation of Emperor Alexander Alexandrovich and Empress Maria Feodorovna from the Moscow Nobility.' As such, this charger served as a bread plate for the welcoming ceremony of *khleb i sol* – bread and salt – performed on the occasion of Tsar Alexander III's coronation in the Moscow Kremlin on 27 May 1883.

28. Punch Bowl *cloisonné* enamel with chrysoprases, garnets, agates, amethysts, 29¹⁴ inches in length, signed with Imperial Warrant mark of Pavel Ovchinnkov, before 1896. The Khalili Family Trust.

The firm of Ovchinnikov was, between 1870 and 1917, the most important silversmithery and enamelry in Russia. The exuberance of this large article, with its intricate *cloisonné* enameling and settings of a profusion of semi-precious stones, is indicative of one line of the firm's production.

29. Hinged Box in the Shape of a Crown enameled silver, decorated with *cloisonné*, 4¼ inches, stamped with initials for Antip Ivanovich Kuzmichev and with 'Made for Tiffany & Co.,' 1887. André Ruzhnikov. With its cross finial serving as a convenient handle, this article illustrates the prevailing practice among jewelers in the late eighteenth and early nineteenth century of acquiring articles created by one firm for retail by another. Fabergé, like Tiffany, also acquired articles crafted by others which he then retailed under his own name.

30. Saltcellar in the Shape of a Peasant Woman with a Sack of Grain silver, with initials of Grigory Loskutov, 4 inches in height, 1887. The State Hermitage Museum.

The third quarter of the 19th century witnessed a burgeoning of peasant themes in Russian art, from Ovchinnikov's large silver group commemorating the Liberation of the Serfs, which earned him a silver medal at the Paris world's fair in 1867, to Sazikov's much lauded 'Dmitri Donskoi Wounded on the Field of Kulikovo', which measured over 10 feet in height and weighed 150 pounds. This article by Loskutov must be regarded within this tradition.

31. Oval Box enameled silver-gilt, 2⅝ inches in length, signed with initials of Maria Semyonova, 1908–17. André Ruzhnikov.
This small box with its simulated beaded lid and floriform decorated sides was created by Maria Semyonova, the owner from 1896 to 1917 of a silverware factory founded by her father in 1852. In 1905 she was employing 100 individuals.

32. Rectangular Box shaded *cloisonné* enamel, 4⅞ inches in length, signed with initials of Feodor Rückert, 1908–17. Private Collection.
Born in France, Rückert, in accordance with a custom of the time, was brought to Russia as a lad of 14 by an aristocratic family and went on to become a famous silversmith in Moscow. He began to work for Fabergé in about 1887 but not exclusively because he continued to create articles such as this box for other retailing opportunities. The lid is decorated with an enamel panel painting of 'The Bride Choosing Her Linen,' after a painting by V. Makovsky.

33. Oblong Box silver-gilt and *cloisonné* enamel, 5 inches in length, attributed to Feodor Rückert, 1908–17. André Ruzhnikov.
The cover is painted *en plein*, meaning that the enamel has been uniformly applied over a relatively large surface, with 'The Warrior at the Crossroads,' after a famous painting by I. Bilibin, framed by a stylized dove and an owl. The reverse is decorated with two imaginary birds.

3

Monumental conception and imposing splendor

Peter Carl Fabergé met the challenges presented by his rival Russian silversmiths and enamelers head on when he decided to open his Moscow branch in 1887, realizing full well that salaries there were 20 percent lower than in St. Petersburg and that he could draw on the talents of highly trained, independent silversmiths. Fabergé's Moscow silver production was prodigious, consisting of tableware, retirement gifts, presentation pieces, and prizes for competitions. Their designs were eclectic in the extreme, with a market-driven preference for the older Pan-Slavic or newly fashionable Neo-Russian idiom, inspired by Russian folk art, as well as for the imported language of Art Nouveau, particularly evident in those articles by Feodor Rückert, when he was not working as an independent.

These silver creations from the Moscow branch of the House of Fabergé have additionally been characterized as both showy and naturalistic, exhibiting a freedom from restraint that was not typical of Russian works. The blend of the old and the new, of the Russian and the foreign, can best be appreciated in the works of art on view in this environment. When compared to that of the competition, the silver oeuvre of the Moscow branch of the House of Fabergé is truly outstanding in quality and made of heavier gauges of silver. Furthermore, all of these works exhibit such an originality of conception and an absence of clichés in their compositions that they have been aptly described as possessed of a 'monumental conception and imposing splendor.'

34. Cigarette Case silver with a sapphire push piece, 4³⁄₈ inches in length, signed with Imperial Warrant mark of Fabergé, 1908–17. John Traina Collection. Here we have an article created by Rückert for Fabergé. The cover is decorated, again *en plein*, with a graphically designed scene of a bear attacking a boyar who holds a drawn sword. The intensity of the scene is conveyed by treating man and beast as waist-length busts, their eyes staring into each other's faces, with the boyar's figure confined to the lower, left-hand corner of the scene, emphasizing his disadvantage in the encounter.

35. *Trompe L'oeil* Tea Caddy Shaped as a Package of Tea silver, 5¹⁄₂ inches in width, with Imperial Warrant mark of Fabergé, before 1899. Private Collection.
Crafted to trick the eye into thinking it is an actual package wrapped in paper and tied with string, this tea caddy's verisimilitude extends to the inclusion of an engraving imitating the design of the wrapping paper, stamped 'K.S. Popov Brothers, tea from China', and a customs band on its rim.

36. Brown Jug silver-mounted earthenware, 11¼ inches, signed with Imperial Warrant mark of Fabergé, before 1899. Michael and Ella Kofman Collection.
This jug is an interesting example of how Fabergé could combine materials of disparate values into an aesthetically pleasing creation. He has mounted a simple brown earthenware jug with silver wrought in the Louis XV-style to great advantage.

37. Decanter silver-mounted glass, 9½ inches, stamped with Imperial Warrant of Fabergé, before 1899. André Ruzhnikov.
Here again Fabergé's creative genius has combined glass and silver into a remarkable article. The tapering, fluted body of the glass vessel is fitted with a silver rim and lidded cover. Its handle is formed as a naturalistically cast and shaped lizard, and it is attached so subtly to the glass that one fails to see its fasteners. The effect is one of a lizard in the wild, about to scurry off in an instant.

38. Carafe silver-mounted glass, 7¹⁄₈ inches, signed with Imperial Warrant mark of Fabergé, 1899–1908. Wartski, London. Whimsically combining the motif of a fish swimming among the waves carved into the glass of the vessel's body with a silver mount in the form of a wolf-fish, one might well imagine the former swimming about on its own when the carafe was filled.

39. Box Shaped as an Egg silver, 5³⁄₈ inches in length, Imperial Warrant mark of Fabergé, 1890–96. Michael and Ella Kofman Collection. Fabergé was a master at accommodating the shape of an egg to any number of articles, from pendants to clocks and even to boxes, as this example demonstrates. Its scrolls and foliage swirling around rock-shaped motifs is indebted to the Rococo-style and are perfectly suited for the curvilinear surfaces they adorn.

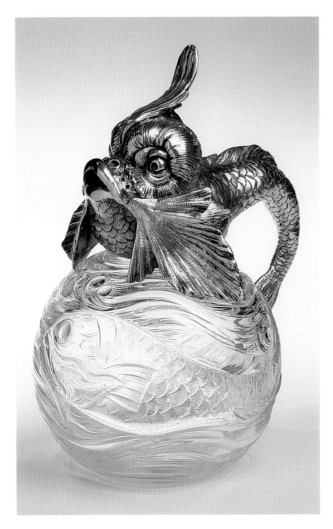

40. Monumental Bogatyr Kovsh silver, silver gilt, and semiprecious stones, 23 inches, marks: Imperial Warrant, 1899–1908. The FORBES Magazine Collection, New York. This monumental kovsh, or scoop, is decorated in the Pan-Slavic style which gained wide-currency in certain Muscovite circles. Its handle is elaborately formed of ancient Russian bogatyrs, or warriors, who look outward by glance or gesture to the horizon beyond. The subject recounts 'The Tale of the Armament of Igor,' a late 12th-century Russian epic poem in which pagan Russian soldiers defeat a young Christian prince from Kiev and his army. The chased figures are clothed in minutely detailed chain mail and, armed with shields and maces, are poised ready to engage the enemy. The massive scale and elaborate craftsmanship of this article, together with its bellicose theme in conjunction with the double-headed eagle appearing at the front, suggest that this particular kovsh was doubtless an imperial gift to a distinguished military regiment or personage. The original sketch for this kovsh has survived and is now in the collections of the State Hermitage Museum.

41. Boris Godunov Desk Set

silver, rock crystal, and *pâte de verre*, 16½ inches in length [the inkwell], marks: Fabergé, Imperial Warrant on all but the seal which bears his initials in Cyrillic. The FORBES Magazine Collection, New York.

This desk garniture was expressly created by Fabergé for the set designer Nikolai Roerich on the occasion of the production of Rimsky-Korsakov's production of Moussorgsky's opera, 'Boris Godunov.' This opera, set in Russia and Poland in the late 16th and early 17th century, is a blend of fact and fiction which recounts the tale of Boris Godunov who, after the death of Ivan the Terrible, assassinates that tsar's son, Dmitri, and rules as regent for Ivan's feeble minded son, Feodor. A false Dmitri then emerges as the pretender to the throne and succeeds in inciting the Russian people to overthrow Boris's regime. He is driven to madness as a result.

The garniture depicts scene 2 of act 4 of that opera. The inkwell portrays a group of landed noblemen who have gathered to discuss the country's fate. Their discussion is interrupted by Prince Shouisky who informs all of the tsar's fragile state of mind. The pen tray represents the distraught Boris, and the hand seal – the expressionless Feodor. The lamp and letter holder represent the conflicting political forces brewing in Russia.

4 The perfectionist and innovator

Whereas the workmasters in the Moscow branch of the House of Fabergé rarely stamped their initials into their articles, those working in St. Petersburg regularly did so. Among the latter was Stephan Wäkeva, a native of Sakkijarvi, Finland. As a proprietor of a workshop, he supplied Fabergé with silver tea services, tankards, and punch bowls. His two sons, Konstantin and Alexander, also worked for the House of Fabergé, Alexander eventually taking over the business upon the death of his father.

Julius Rappoport, a native of the Jewish community in Kaunas province, was a second silversmith, whose forte was crafting superbly modeled animal figures, many of them functional objects serving as salt and pepper shakers, clocks, wine pitchers, and the like. Many of these silver animals served as bellpushes. Their eyes, usually set with red cabochon garnets, functioned as the actual buttons and were ingeniously linked to a simple electrical lever interrupter activated by a metal spring. The complete mechanism was housed in the hollow cavity of the animal, and a single hole, usually drilled on one side, allowed the wires to protrude in order to make the necessary electrical connection.

Rappoport also specialized in silver mounts for various articles crafted of hard stones such as cigarette lighters, matchstrikers, and containers also shaped as animals. Many of these creations display a high degree of realism, miniaturized in the finely worked detail of their fur or plumage. This realism is enhanced by the portrayal of the animal's characteristics.

All these silver animals are universally regarded as masterpieces of the art of silversmithing. And although there is a long tradition behind them, only Fabergé was able to seize upon an established type and, in his own inimitable way as a perfectionist and innovator, transform that type into something uniquely his own. These silver animal creations were priced in their day at the equivalent of $102 to $716.

42. Pitcher in the Shape of a Rabbit silver with gilt interior and ruby eyes, 9¾ inches, stamped with Imperial Warrant mark of Fabergé, 1894. Private Collection. Although there had been a long tradition of creating silver animal sculptures, Fabergé was not interested in perpetuating a cliché; he strove to design these sculptures as luxurious objects which could be used in daily life, and when so used might also serve as interesting table decorations. This pitcher is a case in point. It was formerly in the collection of King Ferdinand of Bulgaria (1861-1948) and family tradition maintains that this pitcher, together with six silver rabbit statuettes in smaller scale, came in one large Fabergé box, now lost. The ensemble was doubtless intended to serve as a table garniture when the pitcher was filled.

43. *Trompe L'oeil* **Saltcellar in the Form of a Radish** silver with gilt interior, 4¾ inches in length, signed Fabergé with initials of Julius Rappoport, before 1899. Private Collection. Julius Rappoport was born in 1851 into a Jewish family of Datnowski, in the province of Kovno, and became Master in 1884 in St. Petersburg. He joined Fabergé's firm about 1890, and thereby gained greater financial security and a larger clientele, but at the loss of his right to sell his articles individually in his own name. Although primarily known for functional articles designed as animals, this wonderful saltcellar was doubtless a conversation piece at table, where it not only dispensed salt but also served as an attractive garniture.

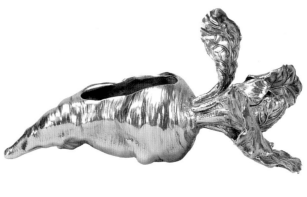

44. Big Bad Wolf Lighter silver, glazed earthenware, wick, 6½ inches, marks: Imperial Warrant, initials of Julius Rappoport, 1899–1908. The FORBES Magazine Collection, New York.
This cigar lighter is representative of the best work of Rappoport who was able to design functional articles in the shape of an array of animals. The beast, wearing a knotted silver kerchief over its red earthenware body, would humorously appear to be smoking the wick when lighted. The entire design was wholly inspired by the character of the big bad wolf in the fairy tale 'Little Red Riding Hood.'

45. Inkwell in the Shape of a Begging Pug Dog silver-mounted burr wood with brown glass eyes, 5⅛ inches, signed Fabergé with initials of the First Silver Artel, 1908-17. Private Collection.
The First Silver Artel was a cooperative that was in operation for about ten years from 1900. Employing about twenty craftsmen, it created articles for Fabergé in silver, such as this example, many utilizing production molds from Rappoport's stock. The round wooden body opens to reveal a silver lined cavity in which ink was stored.

46. Griffin Clock silver-mounted bowenite, 12¼ inches, Imperial Warrant mark of Fabergé with initials of Julius Rappoport, 1896–1908. The Khalili Family Trust. The ingenuity of Fabergé is clearly evident in this article which ostensibly depicts an armed, heraldic griffin advancing with open mouth. Prepared to do battle, it is armed with a raised sword in one paw and a shield, ingeniously shaped as a clock, in the other.

5

Erik Kollin – Fabergé's first chief jeweler

Born the son of a farm laborer in Finland, Erik Kollin began his apprenticeship as a goldsmith in 1852 before obtaining a travel pass to St. Petersburg, where he was enrolled as a goldworker. His career from that point on demonstrates a salient feature of the House of Fabergé, one that sets it apart from its competitors. Peter Carl Fabergé secured the services of workmasters who had previously apprenticed under other craftsmen in his employ. The pattern was established by Erik Kollin who served for ten years as a journeyman in the workshop of August Holmström. Such a practice contributed enormously to the maintenance of corporate continuity. When he was replaced by Michael Perchin, Kollin continued to work until his death as an independent, supplying articles to Fabergé as an outworker.

Kollin's main claim to fame are his replicas of ancient gold jewelry found at Kertch, in the Crimea, created by Greek goldsmiths in the 4th century B.C. and eventually integrated into the imperial collections of the Hermitage. Although such archaeological jewelry had been commonplace in London, Paris, and Rome, it was quite a novelty in Russia, and was hailed in the press as something quite remarkable: 'Mr. Fabergé opens a new era in the art of jewelry.' Fabergé, and through him his workmaster Kollin, was lauded for the very exceptional craftsmanship exhibited by those works. As a result, the House of Fabergé introduced Russia to the concept of artistic jewelry – *bijoux* – as opposed to jewels whose value was based on their precious stones – *joaillerie*. Kollin was to receive a Gold Medal at the Nürnberg International Fine Arts Exhibition in 1885 for his Kertch jewels.

Kollin's oeuvre for the House of Fabergé comprises numerous objects of art, mostly crafted in yellow gold, many of them with reeded surfaces incorporating coins, medals, tigers' claws, and toucans' beaks. His workshop also mounted choice hardstone vessels – *kovshi, charki* and bowls – fashioned from striated agate, jadeite, and purpurine, with elegant gold mounts.

47. Scythian-Style Bracelet
gold, 2^{5}16 inches in length, marks:
initials of Erik Kollin, before
1896. The FORBES Magazine
Collection.
Throughout the course of the
19th century Russian
archaeologists excavated ancient
sites at Kertch in the Crimea.
Among the treasure found were
examples of ancient gold jewelry
created for Scythians, ancient
nomadic dwellers of the Russian
steppes. These treasures were so
popular that Grand Duke
Constantine, an uncle of Tsar
Nicholas II, used to arrange slide
lectures about this material
delivered by distinguished
scholars. All of these treasures
eventually made their way into
the imperial collections of the
Hermitage under the supervision
of Count Sergei Stroganoff. He,
after gaining the permission of
Tsar Alexander III, suggested to
Fabergé that his firm should make
replicas of some of them. Fabergé
took up the suggestion and in
concert with his brother Agathon
and Erik Kollin fashioned a series
of which this gold bangle bracelet
is a part. It features confronted
lion's heads with bared fangs, the
collar of each feline chased with
stylized foliates and pellets. The
collection of these replicas earned
the House of Fabergé a Gold
Medal at the 1882 Pan-Russian
Industrial Exhibition, and the
praise of Tsar Alexander III.

48. Chinese Bowl silver-
mounted shalestone, 2^{1}16 inches in
width, with initials of Erik Kollin,
before 1899. The Woolf Family
Collection.
The genius of Fabergé extended
to embellishing works of art from
other cultures in order to enhance
their aesthetic appeal. In this
particular case, he has taken an
original Chinese bowl to which
he has accommodated a silver
mount, but that mount was
crafted in a style consistent with
the bowl's origin. It is for that
reason that the mount here
simulates bamboo.

49. Easter Egg gold-mounted
agate, 2^{1}16 inches, with initials of
Michael Perchin, before 1899.
Adulf P. Goop Collection.
This bonbonnière in the style of
George II opens by means of a
hinged mount in the form of a
stylized leaf. It was intended as an
Easter gift by virtue of its Cyrillic
inscription – *Khristos Voskres*
(Christ is risen) – within the
opaque white enamel band.

50. Brooch diamond-set gold,
with initials of Erik Kollin.
Private Collection, courtesy Ulla
Tillander-Godenhielm.
Kollin was well-known for his
gold jewelry. This particular
examples features a square center
with a brilliant-set 0.6 carat
diamond.

August Hollming – chief workmaster

The proximity of St. Petersburg, Russia, to Finland helps to explain why almost 30 percent of all goldsmiths working in the Russian capital were Finns or Swedish-Finns. To their number belongs August Hollming, born in Loppi, the son of a bookkeeper. He was initially apprenticed to a goldsmith in Helsinki, where he trained for six years before settling in St. Petersburg as a journeyman. Four years later, in 1880 Hollming qualified as Master, opened his own workshop, and was presumably hired by Fabergé shortly thereafter. He was one of the workmasters whose atelier was located after 1900 in Fabergé's flagship establishment at 24 Bolshaya Morskaya on the third floor. There he trained his eldest son, Väinö, born in 1885, who ran the workshop upon the death of his father in 1913 with Otto Hanhinen, Hollming senior's long-standing assistant. Together with Henrik Wigström, whose work is featured in the last gallery of this exhibition, Hollming was the chief artisan of most of the gold, silver, and enamel cigarette cases created by the House of Fabergé. There are over half a dozen of these articles on view in this environment, several having served as Imperial Presentation gifts.

Hollming's talents as a jeweler can also be profitably gauged by the articles displayed here, created for both men and women. For women there is an extraordinary selection of both gem- and diamond-set brooches, some of which also incorporate enamel work into their designs, and a gem-set platinum watch, the dial of which is surrounded by a band of rubies with a diamond border fitted to a platinum chain bracelet. For men there are examples of cuff links, tie pins, and a remarkable set of diamond-set enameled gold studs.

51. Circular Flower Brooch gem-set with sapphires and diamonds, 1 inch in width, with initials of August Hollming, before 1899. Private Collection.
The flower consists of five petals each set with a sapphire centered by a diamond, while additional diamonds and rubies adorn the scrolling gold stem.

52. Brooch gem-set gold-mounted amethyst with diamonds, 1$\frac{13}{16}$ inches in length, with initials of August Hollming, 1899–1908. Private Collection.
The gem-set ribbon tie forms the focal point of this symmetrically designed brooch with its diamond center, flanked by two hexagonal amethysts surrounded by rose-cut diamonds.

53. Floral Brooch gem-set with diamonds and mecca stones, 1$\frac{9}{16}$ inches in length, with initials of August Hollming, 1899–1908. Private Collection.
Five pale blue oval mecca stones form the petals of this flower head, centered by a brilliant-cut diamond. The curved stem glistens with additional gem-set diamonds.

54. Imperial Presentation Brooch gem-set gold and enamel with diamonds, 1$\frac{1}{4}$ inches in length, with initials of August Hollming, 1908–1917. Private Collection, courtesy A. von Solodkoff.
Intended as an imperial gift, this brooch features an imperial crown set with two sapphires and diamonds on a hexagonal white enamel panel which is symmetrically flanked by openwork filigree squares set with rose-cut diamonds.

55. Imperial Presentation Pendant gem-set amethyst and gold with diamonds and a platinum chain, 2⁷₁₆ inches, with initials of August Hollming, 1908-17. Private Collection, courtesy A. von Solodkoff.

Of openwork design, this pendant is surmounted by an imperial crown of diamonds and amethyst from which are suspended four facetted oval amethysts on rose-cut diamond links with platinum chains.

56. Watch gem-set platinum with diamonds and rubies, ¹⁵₁₆ inches diameter, with initials of August Hollming. Private Collection. This gem-set platinum watch has a dial surrounded by a band of rubies and a diamond border. Its bracelet is of platinum.

57. Cigarette Case jeweled and enameled silver-gilt with diamonds, a ruby and sapphire, 3⁵₈ inches in length, with initials of August Hollming, 1908-17. John Traina Collection.

The principal motif on this article is a centered cap of Monomach, first used as the crown during the coronation in 1613 of Michael Romanov, the first tsar of the dynasty. It became a symbol of Romanov rule during the reign of Nicholas II, particularly during the Tercentenary celebrations of the House of Romanov in 1913. Hollming has ingeniously designed this piece in such a way that the crown appears to radiate as a result of its position on the steel-blue sunburst *guilloché* enamel.

August Holmström – Fabergé's jeweler extraordinaire

Born the son of a master bricklayer in Helsinki, Finland, August Holmström arrived in St. Petersburg, apprenticed as a jeweler, acquired his own workshop, and was subsequently engaged as the principal jeweler for the House of Fabergé under Gustav, continuing under his son Peter Carl. The corporate unity was thereby maintained and further reinforced when Holmström's daughter, Fanny, married another Fabergé workmaster, Oscar Pihl. Their daughter, Alma Theresia Pihl, eventually worked for the House of Fabergé as an accomplished designer. In fact, Holmström executed what connoisseurs consider to be two of the most brilliant of the Fabergé Imperial Easter Eggs based on the designs of his granddaughter, Alma.

Holmström's genius is not apparent in the modest pieces of jewelry which he initially created for Gustav Fabergé, and his reputation has suffered considerably because many of his significant creations fell prey to the Bolsheviks' devastation in the early 1920s.

Nevertheless, as one account makes clear, his work was famous in his lifetime 'for its great precision and exquisite technique: such faultless gem-setting is not to be found even in the works by the best Paris jewelers...[these jewels are unsurpassed] in technique, durability, and finish.'

One can appreciate that comment by examining the small surviving group of exquisite jewels created in the workshop of Holmström. The laurel tiara belonging to the Duke and Duchess of Westminster, mounted in red gold and silver, its leaves finely encrusted with minute diamonds, is but one testament in this environment to the extraordinary skills Holmström possessed as a jeweler.

58. Coronation Box two-color gold, enamel, and diamonds, 3³⁄₄ inches in length, marks: FABERGE, initials of August Holmstrom, before 1896. The FORBES Magazine Collection, New York.

The gold box is applied with a deep gold-hued enamel over *guilloché* sunburst patterns accented by imperial double-headed eagles, and each defined and framed within the lattices of a gold-chased trellis set with diamonds. The center of this box displays the diamond-set monogram of Tsar Nicholas II against an oval panel enameled white with a diamond-set border. This box is one of a series of luxury articles created by the House of Fabergé, which was inspired by the golden, ermine-trimmed robes worn by Tsar Nicholas and Tsarina Alexandra in 1896 during their coronation in Moscow. Tradition maintains that this box was given to Nicholas II by Alexandra.

59. Snowflake Brooch gem-set platinum, gold and enamel with diamonds, 1¹⁄₄ inches in length, by Fabergé. Private Collection.

This brooch was owned by Princess Irène of Prussia, a sister of Tsarina Alexandra Feodorovna, who described it in this way in her jewelry album: 'Brooch, white enamel snowflake of very small diamonds in center – [from] the Grand Duke Serge, Hemmelmark, July 1913.'

The brooch is evocative of the snow flakes in diamond-set platinum which Fabergé also created for Emmanuel Nobel of Sweden, who was the darling of Russia's society ladies. He would often hide these baubles in their dinner napkins as party favors.

60. Pendant gem-set platinum and gold-mounted with diamonds and a sapphire, 2⅝ inches, apparently unmarked, date unknown. Private Collection, courtesy A. von Solodkoff. From the elegant diamond-set ribbon tie are suspended laurel garlands and angular scrolls setting off an oval pink sapphire below.

61. The Grosvenor Tiara gold- and silver-mounted gem-set with diamonds, signed with initials of Fabergé, date unknown. Their Graces the Duke and Duchess of Westminster.

Although not signed, this remarkable tiara comes from the jewelry atelier of August Holmström, who was responsible for some of the greatest jewels ever created by the House of Fabergé. This article was designed as a wreath of myrtle in six groups of diamond-set leaves and diamond berries. Because myrtle was a plant sacred to Venus, the Roman goddess of love, it would seem that this tiara was commissioned to be worn by future Grosvenor brides on their wedding day.

Michael Perchin and Fabergé's most glorious creations

Very little is known about the early training of this son of peasant stock who rose to become one of a handful of native-born Russian jewelers to achieve fame in the House of Fabergé. One learns that he did qualify as a jeweler and eventually accepted Henrik Wigström, who was likewise to become a Fabergé workmaster, into his shop. They were soon joined by Agathon, Peter Carl Fabergé's younger brother, whose brilliants talents served the firm well until his premature death. Although ranging in age from 22 to 24, this triumvirate of Perchin, Wigström, and the younger Fabergé, under the inspirational tutelage of Peter Carl, revolutionized the applied arts scene in Russia.

Peter Carl Fabergé's genius as a choreographer now emerged as he guided this extraordinary team of craftsmen, lead by Perchin, whose expertise was responsible for the appearance of the very first enameled gold objects created by the firm. Perchin's decisive role can be judged by this characterization: 'His personality combined a tremendous capacity for work, profound knowledge of his craft, and persistence in solving certain technical problems.'

Although earlier passed over in silence, recent scholarship now suggests that Perchin himself was the author of the First Imperial Easter Egg, created by the House of Fabergé. This article was commissioned in 1885, and stands at the beginning of a tradition that was to last until the fall of tsarist Russia. That first Egg is shown in this exhibition which, interestingly enough, also contains the very last Imperial Easter Egg crafted by the House of Fabergé.

During his tenure as head workmaster, which he attained in 1886, Perchin was responsible for some of the most glorious creations of the House of Fabergé. This environment alone contains more than 125 of Perchin's masterful creations, including several Imperial Easter Eggs, which reveal his extraordinary talents.

62. Art Nouveau Compass
gem-set gold-mounted and
sapphires, 1½ inches in diameter,
with initials of Michael Perchin,
1899-1908. Private Collection.
This compass is ingeniously
designed as a watch case, with
applied and chased water lilies on
both sides. Its cover is gem-set
with two star sapphires.

63. Rectangular Frame three-
color gold and enamel rock crystal
with rubies, 3⁷⁄₁₆ inches in height,
signed Fabergé, with initials of
Michael Perchin, before 1899.
Private Collection, courtesy A.
von Solodkoff.
Perchin has created a perfect
illusion of a picture frame floating
in space by ingeniously and
imperceptibly attaching its gem-
set gold elements to the
rectangular rock-crystal panel. The
frame consists of four staffs of
Maenads, mythological female
followers of Dionysos, Greek god
of wine, applied with symbols of
music and decorated with floral
garlands suspended from rubies.
The photograph is that of Grand
Duke Frederick Francis III of
Mecklenburg-Schwerin.

64. Square Box gem-set enamel
and gold-mounted nephrite and a
large diamond, 1⁹⁄₁₆ inches in
length, signed Fabergé with
initials of Michael Perchin, before
1899. Private Collection, courtesy
A. von Solodkoff.
The cover of this tiny box is
decorated in the Renaissance style
with a large rose-cut diamond
serving as its handle.

65. Weather-frog Bellpush
silver-gilt enamel hardstone with diamonds and a garnet, 3¼ inches, signed Fabergé with initials of Michael Perchin, 1899-1908. The Hubel Collection.

Perchin has designed this weather-frog bell push as a fanciful terrarium consisting of a circular base supported by three ball feet which serves to anchor the bell-shaped rock-crystal cover. Within, a nephrite frog with diamond eyes perches on a ladder beneath a finial in the form of a garnet-set silver-gilt calyx. The ingenuity of the design camouflages the mechanism which triggered the bell push when depressed.

This article was sold to the Imperial Cabinet on December 1, 1900, for the sum of 125 roubles, just over $60, and was given by Tsar Nicholas II to his cousin, Prince George of Greece and Denmark.

66. Louis XVI Snuffbox gold and enamel, 3¼ inches in length, marks: initials of Joseph Etienne Blerzy, 1777. The FORBES Magazine Collection, New York.

67. Louis XVI-style Snuffbox
gold, enamel, diamonds and pearls, 3¼ inches in length, marks: FABERGE, with initials of Michael Perchin, before 1896. The FORBES Magazine Collection, New York.

This earlier snuffbox is a creation of Blerzy, a Parisian 18th-century goldsmith who also worked in Russia. He was one of the most prolific makers of this type of popular 18th-century article. The example here features an enamel plaque with a classical scene depicting the family of Darius III, king of Persia, at the feet of Alexander the Great. Alexander had just defeated Darius, who, in his desire to escape, abandoned both his camp and his family.

Alexander entered the camp and chanced upon the king's abandoned family who entreated Alexander for mercy. This snuffbox was owned by Tsarina Catherine the Great and remained in the imperial collections where it was greatly admired by Tsar Alexander III.

The tsar held the snuffbox in such high esteem that he issued a challenge to his Russian craftsmen stating that they did not possess the technical skills to equal those of the French master goldsmiths of the 18th century.

Fabergé took up the challenge and together with his brother Agathon and Michael Perchin created the second snuffbox which was visibly finer than that made by Blerzy. The gold of the Fabergé creation was more regular because it had been engine-turned, its enamel was less porous. Fabergé substituted a scene in

grisaille, or predominantly gray tones, of Venus and Cupid and surrounded it with a border trimmed by diamonds, green enamel foliage and seed pearls.

Tsar Alexander III was so thrilled with this snuffbox that he ordered both – the original by Blerzy and the second by Fabergé – to be displayed side by side in the Hermitage as a tribute to the extraordinary achievement of Russian craftsmanship.

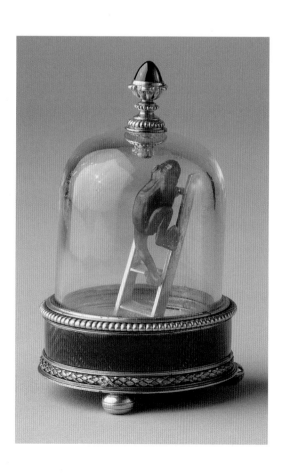

68. Mantle Clock silver-gilt mounted nephrite, 11 inches, by Fabergé, before 1899. Private Collection.

One can tell the time by the head of the snake which points to a rotating dial with Roman chapters near the neck of the urn-shaped clock. It is surmounted by a two-color gilt bouquet of lilies and carnations, together with a cluster of roses. The clock was presented to Dr. Johann Georg Metzger by Tsar Alexander III in December 1893.

Dr. Metzger, a Dutch citizen and physician specializing in therapeutic gymnastics, was summoned by the tsar to St. Petersburg for a second time in 1892 to attend to a back injury suffered by his daughter, Grand Duchess Olga Alexandrovich, in the Borki railway accident (in which the tsar himself is said to have supported the collapsed ceiling of the derailed imperial carriage as his family escaped to safety). For services rendered on this occasion the doctor was given a generous honorarium of 30,000 roubles, the equivalent of $15,000, as well as this clock.

69. Elephant in the Renaissance Style jeweled and enameled gold with diamonds, rubies, and an emerald, 1⁷⁄₁₆ inches, date unknown, signed Fabergé. Private Collection.

Despite its small size, this elephant is finely detailed, from its mahout (elephant-driver) seated on its head to the diamond-set turret on its back, which rests on a diamond and ruby studded saddle cloth. The elephant itself stands on an emerald, with an enameled runner between its feet. The elephant, an emblem of the Danish royal house, is so consummately crafted and lavishly adorned that it appears to have had a royal connection, particularly since Tsarina Maria Feodorovna, the wife of Alexander III, had been born Princess Dagmar of Denmark. The suggestion is given further credence by the observation that this article, like others made for the tsarist imperial family by the House of Fabergé, lacks an inventory number. It seems logical to argue that the elephant was a surprise for an early Imperial Easter Egg.

It cannot, however, be associated with the elephant surprise of the Diamond Trellis Egg since that article is described as a clockwork.

70. The Apple Blossom Egg jeweled, enameled gold-mounted nephrite with diamonds, 5¹⁄₂ inches, engraved signature of Fabergé, initials of Michael Perchin, 1899–1908. Adulf P. Goop Collection.

The egg is so named because the nephrite, or Siberian jade, is mounted in gold, the four legs of which represent apple trees from which a network of branches encircle the egg itself. The opaque white enamel apple blossoms have centers of pink-foiled rose-cut diamonds.

Fabergé created Easter eggs not only for Tsars Alexander III and his son and successor, Nicholas II, but for other wealthy clients, such as Alexander Kelch, the so-called 'king of Russian gold mines'. Kelch commissioned this and six other eggs successively as gifts for his wife, Barbara, who was herself extremely wealthy. Sharing with their Imperial counterparts a high level of technical sophistication, but being of slightly larger size, the Kelch Easter eggs were originally thought to have been Imperial Easter eggs when they first appeared on the Paris market, where they were sold after Barbara Kelch fled from Russia in the wake of the Revolution of 1917.

71. First Egg varicolored gold, enamel and rubies, 2½ inches in length [the shell], not marked but attributed to Erik Kollin, date unknown, presented at Easter 1895. The FORBES Magazine Collection, New York.

This is the very first Imperial Easter Egg created by Fabergé for Tsar Alexander III who presented it to his wife, Tsarina Maria Feodorovna, on Easter 1885. It stands at the head of a tradition which was to continue under their son and heir, Nicholas II, and end abruptly with the Russian Revolution of 1917.

At first glance the plain matte white enameled egg appears to be singularly uninteresting, but one should never judge a book by its cover. It contained many marvels within. The shell twists open to reveal a removable gold yolk which in turn can be opened to reveal a varicolored gold hen with realistically engraved feathers and ruby-set eyes. The plump fowl sits inside a suede and gold nest stippled to simulate straw. A gentle push upward underneath the hen's beak enabled the tsarina to extract from its hollow belly two final surprises – a tiny ruby egg-shaped pendant suspended inside an exquisite diamond-set replica of her imperial crown. The whereabouts of these treasures is not known.

72. The Pamiat Azova Imperial Easter Egg jeweled, gold-mounted bloodstone with diamonds and a ruby, 3¹¹⁄₁₆ inches in length [the shell], signed Fabergé with initials of Michael Perchin, before 1899. Kremlin Armory Museum.

The surprise of this egg is a miniature replica of the vessel HMS *Pamiat Azova* ('The Memory of the Azov'), named in honor of an earlier Russian battleship, HMS *Azov* which saw action in the Battle of Navarino in 1827, and was the first vessel in the Russian navy to be awarded the flag of St. George.

In 1890 Tsar Alexander III arranged for his son and heir, Nicholas, to sail to the East on the *Pamiat Azova*, accompanied by trusted officers and his brother and cousin. The journey lasted more than nine months, and is commemorated by this Easter egg. The prominence given to the ruby of its push piece is intentional, its blood-red color recalling the wound delivered by a sword-wielding, disgruntled samurai to the head of Nicholas during his visit to Japan.

When this egg was exhibited in 1900 at the Paris world's fair, together with 14 other Imperial Easter Eggs, it was singled out and criticized for being old-fashioned and out-of-step with the times – its overtly Louis XV-style was seen to be incompatible with the then prevailing Art Nouveau aesthetic.

7

Fabergé's magical menagerie and fabulous flowers

Peter Carl Fabergé loved animals, particularly birds. In fact, he is reported to have taught a starling to whistle a melody from Gounod's opera *Faust*. This love was extended to his animal figures, virtually all of which were created from semiprecious stones indigenous to Russia. In selecting stones for particular animals, one senses that Peter Carl was subconsciously reaffirming Aristotle's dictum that 'everything desires to maintain its own nature.' His craftsmen, particularly Peter Kremlev and Peter Derbyshev, skillfully took into consideration the veining and colors of the various stones, and sometimes even their shapes, so that those characteristics could be artfully transformed into either correspondingly shaped parts of the animals or their fur. Some of these animals are very naturalistic in appearance and others, as if conforming to Peter Carl Fabergé's own wit, appear to be caricatures. Many of these same qualities can be appreciated in the hardstone human figures which the firm also created. An anecdote connected with these animal sculptures reflects the human, tender side of Fabergé, who reveled in the joy of life and in the delight of living. It seemed that it was with mixed feelings of wonder and anxiety that clients in his shop would watch Peter Carl Fabergé settle their small children on the floor, surrounding them with a number of his exquisite, but not unbreakable, animal carvings.

The miniature flowers created by the House of Fabergé were exceedingly popular in his time, despite the fact that their average cost was ten times that of a hardstone animal sculpture. Their popularity was due in no small part to the love of flowers among Russians, who might regard these miniatures metaphorically as bringing summer into an otherwise cold and dark St. Petersburg winter. They are also evocative of *The Waltz of the Flowers* by Fabergé's contemporary, Tchaikovsky. Small wonder, then, that connoisseurs rank these miniature floral arrangements among the most beautiful of all the creations of the House of Fabergé.

73. Owl agate and diamonds, 2 inches, by Fabergé. Joan and Melissa Rivers.

74. Parasol Handle Surmounted by a Frog diamond-set, enameled, gold-mounted nephrite, 3½ inches, by Fabergé. Joan and Melissa Rivers.

75. Sow pink aventurine quartz with rose-cut diamonds and gold mounts, 2 inches in length. H.M. King Carl XVI Gustav of Sweden.

76. Hippopotamus obsidian with rose-cut diamond eyes, 2 inches in length. Private Collection, courtesy Ulla Tillander-Godenhielm.

77. Rhinoceros bowenite with ruby eyes, 6½ inches in length. From The Castle Howard Collection.

78. Elephant chalcedony with rose-cut diamond eyes, 1¾ inches, From The Castle Howard Collection. This selection of hard-stone animals is representative of the approach toward wild life that Fabergé took, attempting on the one hand to match the material used with their coats while at the same time striving to capture the essential characteristics of the species depicted. The use of diamonds and rubies heighten the effect, and contribute to the precious charm these creatures still exude to this day.

79. Cranberry Spray silver-gilt mounted hardstone, standing in a rock crystal pot simulating water content, 5½ inches, by Fabergé. Joan and Melissa Rivers.

80. Alpine Strawberry gem-set enameled gold and hardstone with diamond and pearls, set in a rock crystal pot simulating water content, 4¼ inches, by Fabergé. The Woolf Family Collection.

81. Conical Vase Parlant by Gallé with silver mount signed Fabergé with initials of Julius Rappoport, before 1899, 8¹⁄₁₆ inches. The State Hermitage Museum.

It has been suggested that this vase was one of several work of art by Emile Gallé acquired by Tsarina Alexandra Feodorovna during her 1896 visit to relatives in Darmstadt, Germany. Its Fabergé stand was commissioned by the Imperial Cabinet in St. Petersburg on February 21, 1898 at a cost of 70 roubles, or $35.

The vase is etched around the lip with quotations from Maurice Maeterlinck, one of Gallé's favorite poets: 'Végétations de Symboles' and 'Palmes lentes de mes désirs. Nénuphars mornes des plaisirs. Mousses froides, lianes molles...' Gallé first began incorporating quotations into the designs of his vases in 1884, thereby imparting a symbolist character to these works of art, which became known as *vases parlants*, or 'speaking vases.' Whereas earlier critics condemned these floral studies as nothing more than colored photographs, more enlightened connoisseurs consider them the most beautiful of all Fabergé's creations. Highly prized in their own day, and priced at an average of 1,000 roubles – the equivalent of $500 or about 10 times that of one of the firm's hardstone animal carvings – these floral studies resonate with a Russian fascination for flowers. Rimsky Korsakov's 'The Invisible City of Kitesch', for example, contains a passage early in the third act in which, as the orchestra spins a dark and fragile web of magic, separate and distinct bell notes ring out with crystal clarity; they suggest very vividly the sudden miraculous appearance of flowers in an enchanted forest. Fabergé's floral studies belong to a likewise enchanted garden.

Fabergé's adamant insistence that his miniature floral creations were absolutely devoid of any symbolic overtones requires comment, inasmuch as many intellectuals in the late 19th century were preoccupied with flowers. His contemporary Maeterlinck wrote *The Intelligence of the Flowers* and *News of Spring and Other Nature Studies*. Maeterlinck further argues that gathering flowers is a criminal act because in so doing one murders them for their soul. In my view, Fabergé must surely have been aware of this 19th-century intellectual fascination with flowers, as is confirmed by the observation that Tsarina Alexandra acquired several *vases parlants* created by Gallé, one of which is inscribed with quotations from Maeterlinck and mounted in silver by Fabergé. From the tsarina's demonstrable interest in flowers,

and her acquisition of such vases in Darmstadt where her brother's interest in the avant-garde would certainly have sparked discussion about the symbolists' approach to the floral kingdom, it can be suggested that she had ample opportunity to discuss such topics with Fabergé. His vigorous refusal to ascribe symbolic overtones to his floral creations would appear to suggest that some were attempting to relate his creations to that century's intellectual fascination with the floral kingdom. And since his biographers affirm that Fabergé was never serious, his floral studies should be accepted at face value: as enchanting echoes of nature's beauty, divorced from the floral animism of the symbolists.

82. Frame Shaped as a Pansy
jeweled, gold-mounted with diamonds, standing in a tapering rock-crystal pot simulating partial water content, $6^{1}8$ inches, signed Fabergé with initials of Michael Perchin, 1899–1908. The Kremlin Armory Museum.
Given Tsarina Alexandra Feodorovna's passion for flowers ('I have begun painting flowers, as alas have had to leave singing and playing as too tiring'), it is not surprising to learn that this remarkable frame was given to her as a 10th anniversary gift by her husband, Tsar Nicholas II, for which reason it is engraved with the Roman numeral X, as well as with the names of their five children – Grand Duchesses Olga, Tatiana, Marie, Anastasia, and Tsarevich Alexei. The petals open to reveal their miniature portraits.

Fabergé – master marketer

An astute businessman, Peter Carl Fabergé realized the value of marketing his articles. He once remarked, 'The firm's large turnover enables it to sell its wares at very reasonable prices, which are kept as low as is commensurate with maintaining the high quality of the work.' In today's currency, one could find items in his shop ranging in price from a few dollars for the smallest bauble to objects retailing for hundreds of thousands of dollars. Fabergé habitually maintained an inventory which was as varied as possible. His selection of offerings might include everything for smokers from cigarette cases to matchstick holders and ashtrays; handles for canes, walking sticks, and parasols; fans, opera glasses, combs, snuff bottles, knitting needles, electric bell pushes; desk accessories such as pen holders, blotting-pad holders, stamp dispensers; candlesticks, coffee and tea services, garnitures, and full-scale pieces of furniture. 'We accept orders for the above-mentioned objects, as well as [orders for] prizes for societies organizing racing and jumping events, and we send out-of-town customers designs, estimates and illustrated price lists on request.'

He issued catalogues, he said, because clients 'live in the provinces, have no opportunity of visiting our premises personally and of seeing for themselves our rich selection of goods.' He guaranteed to take back or exchange individual pieces provided that they had not been made to order, that they were not damaged, and that they had been purchased fairly recently.

The House of Fabergé did serve an elite clientele but offered similar merchandise at prices attractive to what one might call the middle class. Fabergé may have sold only one Imperial Easter Egg a year to Tsar Alexander III, but imagine how many parasol handles, cigarette cases, and picture frames were sold to walk-up clients who desired to own an object from the exclusive House of Fabergé!

83. Deep, Rectangular Tray
silver-mounted brown-glazed ceramic, 6¼ inches in length, with initials of Anders Nevalainen, before 1899. Private Collection. The ceramic tray has been artfully mounted with a silver mount, the handles of which are in the shape of laurel wreaths and ribbons.

84. Miniature Vodka Cup
jeweled silver and enamel with a moonstone, 1⅝ inches, stamped Fabergé, 1899-1908. Private Collection.
The design consists of a bowl on a beaded foot and a handle in the form of two entwined serpents attached to a bracket set with a moonstone.

85. Art Nouveau Cigarette Case gold-mounted palisander wood with emerald push piece, 3¼ inches, signed Fabergé with initials of Johann Victor Aarne, before 1899. John Traina Collection.
A simple but very elegant interpretation of the floral forms of Art Nouveau, the design contrasts the wood with its gold mount and focuses one's attention on the emerald push piece.

86. Standing Thermometer enameled silver-gilt and maple wood, 4⁷⁄₈ inches, marks: FABERGE, with initials of Johann Victor Aarne, 1896–1908. The FORBES Magazine Collection, New York.

Fabergé's product lines were extended to include optics and instruments such as this thermometer. It is set with a rectangular panel surmounted by a ribbon-tied cresting.

87. Circular Bellpush silver-mounted mahogany with a moonstone, 2 inches in length, signed Fabergé with initials of Hjalmar Armfeldt, 1899–1908. Private Collection, courtesy A. von Solodkoff.

A Finn who became a journeyman in 1891, Armfeldt acquired the workshop of goldsmith Viktor Aarne, with its 20 goldsmiths and three apprentices, for the sum of 8,000 roubles, but was given to understand that the Fabergé family expected him to maintain the high standards set by his predecessor.

88. Tankard in the 18th-Century Style silver with coins, 4¹⁄₈ inches, signed Fabergé with initials of Anders Nevalainen, 1899–1903. The State Hermitage Museum.

Standing on three ball feet, the cover of this tankard is applied with a 50-kopeck coin of Catherine the Great, its sides with three 10-kopeck coins of Tsarina Elisabeth I. The article is a contemporary rendition of an 18th-century idiom, not only in its shape but also in its imitation of a Russian 18th-century tradition of decorating jewelry and metalwork with coins and medals.

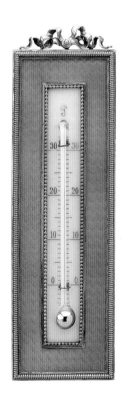

89. Cigarette Case platinum and silver-gilt with a gold-mounted garnet thumb piece, 3⅜ inches in length, signed Fabergé with initials of Anders Nevalainen, before 1899. Courtesy A La Vieille Russie.

The case displays an interesting array of decorative elements including the use of the alphabet for a monogram BK, an applied initial K in a roundel, the word 'Amico,' and the facsimile signature of Count Shuralov. Additionally one finds a bar of music, a fence with a cat, a diamond-set dachshund, and a touring car.

The monogram BK and the initial may be identified with Barbara Kelch, one of Fabergé's wealthiest clients, for whom the firm created seven magnificent Easter eggs. This particular case was presumably a gift from her to Count Pavel Petrovich Shuvalov, a well-known collector and patron of the arts.

90. Triptych Desk Clock and Photograph Frame enameled silver-gilt and pearls, 8¼ inches wide [when opened], signed Fabergé with initials of Viktor Aarne, 1899–1908. Private Collection.

The three panels are supported by four stands acting as hinges, each in the form of a thyrsos – a floral staff carried by Maenads in rites associated with Dionysos, the Greek god of wine. The bezel is framed by pearls.

91. Elongated Octagonal Pin jeweled platinum with diamonds, rubies, sapphires, topazes, demantoids, garnets, and emeralds, 1¹¹⁄₁₆ inches in length, signed Fabergé, designed by Alma Theresia Pihl. The Woolf Family Collection.

The frame is set with rose-cut diamonds supporting an openwork panel simulating *petit point* set with an array of gemstones to form a floral study. This article is based on a design by Alma Theresia Pihl that appears in the stock book of Albert Holmström. The presence of these two individuals on the staff of Fabergé accounts for his success in maintaining corporate continuity, achieved in part by maintaining familial continuity as well. Workmaster August Holmström's daughter, Fanny, married Knut Oskar Pihl. Pihl trained under Holmström. Fanny and Knut Pihl's daughter, Alma Theresia Pihl, joined the firm as an excellent designer, and was responsible for the design of this pin which appears in the stock book of Albert Holmström, her paternal uncle.

Moscovite *objets d'art*

The Moscow branch of the House of Fabergé opened in 1887 and was initially headed by A. Bowe, whom Fabergé held in high esteem, often referring to him as 'my assistant and first manager.' The workshop was divided into two departments, one for jewelry and the other for gold and silver objects. Some of Fabergé's closest associates were somewhat disparaging in their assessment of the silver production created by the firm's Moscow branch. One individual even went so far as to state that 'the way the Moscow branch is run is an attempt to exploit the genius of Fabergé on a commercial basis.' This negative assessment can now be revised in light of the extraordinary collection displayed here of some 75 *objets d'art* in gold and silver created by the Moscow branch of the House of Fabergé. Their number includes cigarette cases, picture frames, perpetual calendars, bell pushes, scent bottles, a pin cushion, a barometer, a letter opener, vessels and bowls, boxes and cases, a clock, and an array of jewelry including brooches, pendants, bracelets, and finger rings.

Surveying this varied array of articles, one finds that their designs are in fact highly original. The best of these are in an Art Nouveau idiom and were created before 1899. This selection also contains a most interesting cigarette case in the Aesthetic style.

**92. Art Nouveau Fob Key
Chain on a Black Ribbon**
gold with a single baguette
sapphire, 2½ inches in length,
signed Fabergé, 1908–17.
Private Collection, New York.
This article is chased with a
vintage racing motor car.

93. Art Nouveau Pendant
gold with a diamond, 1 inch
in length, signed with Imperial
Warrant mark of Fabergé,
1908–17. Private Collection.
The pendant is cast with a male
head and a male nude against a
drapery backdrop.

94. Souvenir Cigarette Case
silver with a garnet push piece,
4 inches in length, stamped with
Imperial Warrant, 1908-17. John
Traina Collection.
A marvelous assortment of
seemingly disparate motifs are
applied to the side of this plain
case, including a procession of
three elephants of progressively
different sizes, flags, jetons, and the
signatures 'Mama' and 'Mavrika.'

95. Cigarette Case enameled
silver-gilt with diamond push
piece, 3¼ inches in length,
stamped with Imperial Warrant,
before 1899. John Traina
Collection.
The purple *guilloché* enamel of this
case is applied with laurel swags
and opaque white enamel zig-zags
to achieve a harmonious
integration of rectilinear and
curvilinear forms.

96. Cigarette Case *plique-à-jour* enamel and gold, 3¾ inches in length, stamped with Imperial Warrant mark of Fabergé, 1899–1908. Private Collection. Art Nouveau in inspiration, the design of this case relies upon four blue-and-white dragonflies rendered in an enameling technique termed *plique-à-jour*. This technique has often been described by analogy with stained glass because the enamel is not backed, and this accounts for its intense color. In fact each of the separate enameled sections are treated like gemstones set within a collet, or flange, consisting of the main framework of the object. It is an extremely difficult technique to master and was rarely used by Fabergé. Its appearance on this object reveals the virtuosity of his Moscow workshop.

This article is inscribed 'For my darling Ernie from Nikky ad Alix, Xmas 1900,' and was given by Tsar Nicholas II and Tsarina Alexandra to her brother, Grand Duke Ernest Louis of Hesse and the Rhine. The grand duke, an artist himself, founded an artists' colony and was deeply involved with what has become known as Darmstadt Art Nouveau.

97. Scent Flask gold-mounted enameled nephrite, 3⅛ inches in length, signed Fabergé, 1899-1908. Chevalier Maurice Mizzi Collection.
This article is naturalistically shaped as a cucumber.

98. Bellpush gem-set silver with rubies and emeralds, 5¾ inches in length, with Imperial Warrant mark of Fabergé. Private Collection, New York.
In the Art Nouveau style, this article is in the shape of a butterfly with a female head wearing a ruby-set diadem. Each of the wings are set with gold-mounted emeralds.

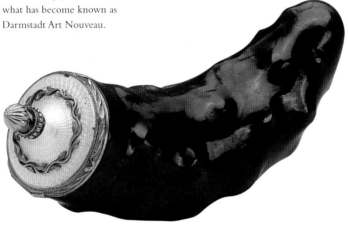

The house of Fabergé and religious art

Peter Carl Fabergé's distant relatives were French Huguenots who were forced into exile and compelled to change their last name in order to conceal their origins when King Louis XIV revoked the terms of the Treaty of Nantes in 1685. Around 1800, Peter Carl's paternal grandfather reverted to the family name of Fabergé and settled in Russia thanks to the enlightened policy of religious toleration espoused by Russia's Tsarina, Catherine the Great.

Still, the Russian society into which Peter Carl Fabergé was born was dominated by the Russian Orthodox Church. One recalls that Tsar Alexander III and his son and successor, Nicholas II, were crowned as rulers of Russia in religious ceremonies conducted in Moscow. The marvelous Imperial Easter Eggs for which the House of Fabergé is justly famous were gifts on the occasion of this most religious holiday within the liturgical calendar of the Russian Orthodox Church.

Members of the imperial family and the aristocracy habitually commissioned religious articles from Fabergé. Henrik Wigström, one of Fabergé's workmasters whose oeuvre is featured in the last gallery of this exhibition, created an icon on the occasion of the marriage of Prince Felix Yusupov to Princess Irina Alexandrovna, a niece of Tsar Nicholas II. That icon is on view in this gallery. Fabergé's competitors were likewise called upon to create liturgical articles for devotional purposes. Many of these works were often submitted to periodic exhibitions and were judged against works by other craftsmen. For example, a Gospel cover, created by Pavel Ovchinnikov, a contemporary of Fabergé, was highly acclaimed at the Pan-Slavic Exhibition of 1882. Several icons by Ovchinnikov can be seen in this gallery.

99. The Yusupov Icon quatrefoil gold and enamel, 1⁵⁄₁₆ inches, with signature of Fabergé and initials of Henrik Wigström, 1908–17. Private Collection, courtesy A. von Solodkoff.

The date engraved on this small icon is that of the wedding of Prince Felix Yusupov, Count Sumarokov-Elston, to Princess Irina Alexandrovna of Russia, eldest daughter of Grand Duke Alexander Michaelovitch and Grand Duchess Xenia Alexandrovna, herself the daughter of Tsar Alexander III and sister of Tsar Nicholas II. Prince Felix is said to have worn this icon on his person. Their wedding has been hailed as the last great society event in imperial Russia before the outbreak of World War I. The groom was later to mastermind the assassination of Rasputin, and incurred the wrath of the tsar despite being married to the tsar's niece.

100. Triptych Icon silver-gilt and *cloisonné* enamel, 12½ inches, the mount attributed to Ivan Khlebnikov. André Ruzhnikov. The icon features St. Nicholas the Miracle Worker flanked to the left by St. Alexander Nevsky and to the right by St. Mary Magdalen. The reverse bears a presentation inscription 'To His Imperial Highness Heir Apparent Nicholas Alexandrovich from the Security Service of the Moscow Bourgeois Society, May 1886.' The saints represented are the patron saints of Tsarevich Nicholas and of his parents, Tsar Alexander III and Tsarina Maria Feodorovna.

101. Triptych Icon silver-mounted, 19¼ inches, initials of Dmitri Smirnov, 1908-17. André Ruzhnikov. Each of the side panels and the central panel are surmounted by onion-shaped domes with Russian Orthodox crosses. The central panel depicts Christ Pantocrator, the left panel St. Nicholas the Miracle Worker and the right the Guardian angel.

The reverse is inscribed, 'To his Imperial Majesty Emperor Nicholas Alexandrovich – In Memory of His Unforgettable Visit of the Don and Novocherekassk/In the tumultuous year/Dedicated to the Last Drop of Blood/Clergy of the Don, December 4, 1914,' and refers to the Russian desire for victory in World War I.

Russian competition and collaboration

As an international capital catering to royals and aristocrats alike, St. Petersburg in 1889 was home to 52 jewelry firms, each vying with the others for patronage. Their number included the House of Bolin, which is not only one of the oldest firms specializing in jewelry and silverware but also one of the few that still remains in the hands of one and the same family. Founded by the German-born jeweler Andreas Roempler in St. Petersburg as early as 1790, the firm was renamed for one of his sons-in-law, Carl Edvard Bolin.

The House of Bolin became Fabergé's main Russian competitor from the 1890s, when it created most of the large pieces of jewelry required by the court. Nevertheless both establishments did collaborate on occasion for the good of Russia, as when in 1906 Fabergé and Bolin attempted to purchase the collection of treasures put up for sale by the imperial court in order to alleviate the debt caused by the Russo-Japanese war. Although they failed – their offer was topped by a foreign competitor – their motive was noble, because they desired to retain those jewels in Russia.

Such collaboration among seeming rivals was not unusual in St. Petersburg at the time. Tillander was a St. Petersburg establishment owned and operated by Alexander Tillander, father and son. The father came to St. Petersburg from Finland at the age of 11 and became an independent goldsmith at the age of 21, selling his work to others, including Bolin. The Austrian Karl Hahn founded his firm in 1873. Upon his death, it was taken over first by his widow and then by his son, Dmitri Hahn, who employed the goldsmith/jeweler Carl Carlovich Blank. When Dmitri Hahn died in 1911, his firm and premises were taken over by Alexander Tillander. At that time, Carl Blank worked independently.

102. Cigarette Case enameled silver, 3 inches in length, signed Shanks and Bolin, 1887. Private Collection.

The front is decorated with two *putti* sitting on a floral garland.

103. Oval Brooch gem-set gold with diamonds, a sapphire and a ruby, 1½ inches in width, signed with initials of Carl Blank. Private Collection.

The design of oblong scrolling foliage is set with diamonds.

104. Miniature Easter Egg gem-set gold with diamonds and rubies, ⅝ inch, signed with initials of Friedrich Koechli, before 1899. The Woolf Family Collection.

The body is formed of two conjoined fleur-de-lys tied with rose-cut diamonds and set with rubies at intervals.

105. Oval *Charka* gold-mounted pearl-set agate 2⅞ inches, with initials of Frederick Koechli, before 1896. Private Collection.

The footed vessel is designed with a mythological bird with chased outstreched wings serving as its handle. Its presentation inscription in French may be translated, 'to Arthur and Alexander, a souvenir from your friends, the Kandinskys, father and son, 1892.'

106. Swan Brooch gem-set and enameled gold, 1⅝ inches wide, signed with initials of Feodor Lorie, 1896-1908. Private Collection.

The contours of the brooch take the form of the swan's outstretched wings; its beak holds a brilliant-cut diamond.

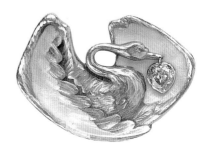

Louis Comfort Tiffany

The American Louis Comfort Tiffany, like Peter Carl Fabergé, was a consummate artist-designer who immeasurably enriched the art of his generation. Both rarely used precious stones and relied upon diamonds for decorative effect rather than to enhance the value of the article being produced. Nevertheless the two firms exhibited together only once at the international exhibition staged in Paris in 1900. Although they often sold to the same clients, their competition was never outwardly hostile.

107. Favrile Vase silver-mounted, the glass signed with initials of Tiffany. Collection Eric Streiner, New York.
The body of the Favrile glass vase of compressed spherical shape is frosted and carved with swirling flutes and hand-carved flowers painted in pink and green.

108. Scarab Tie Pin gold-mounted iridescent blue Favrile glass, 2½ inches in length, the scarab by Tiffany, 1908-10. Collection Eric Streiner, New York.
The scarab in ancient Egyptian culture was thought to propel the sun across the sky and served as a resurrection symbol.

109. Pair of Cufflinks shaped gold, ¾ inches in length, by Tiffany, about 1910. Eric Streiner Collection, New York.
Each of these shaped oval cuff links is chased with three fruit motifs.

110. Necklace platinum-mounted moonstones and sapphires, 20 inches in length, by Tiffany, about 1915. Collection Eric Streiner, New York.
The platinum-mounted moonstone and Montana sapphire necklace has a central oval moonstone surrounded by triple clusters of sapphires.

81

Louis Cartier

The relationship of Louis Cartier, a Frenchman, with the House of Fabergé was often adversarial. Cartier reached the decision to become one of Fabergé's fiercest competitors after he had been impressed by the beauty of 15 Fabergé Imperial Easter Eggs exhibited at the Paris world's fair in 1900, the very year that he and his father opened their elegant establishment in Paris. In time, Cartier's enamels would appear to be stronger than those of Fabergé and his color combinations more intense. He even fashioned a violet and white enameled Imperial Easter Egg which was offered to Tsar Nicholas II on the occasion of the official visit of French President Roussel to Russia.

'Clearly if you compare my things with those of such firms as Tiffany, Boucheron and Cartier, of course you will find that the value of theirs is greater than of mine. As far as they are concerned, it is possible to find a necklace in stock for one and a half million roubles. But of course these people are merchants and not artist-jewelers. Expensive things interest me little if the value is merely in so many diamonds or pearls,' was how Fabergé regarded the situation.

In 1909 Louis Cartier traveled to Russia to participate in a charity bazaar organized by Grand Duchess Maria Pavlovna, and the jealousy and antagonism of local jewelers, led no doubt by Fabergé and Bolin, against Cartier reached their peak. Cartier was accused of tax and custom's duty evasions and discrepancies in hallmarking, and his articles were temporarily seized. Shortly thereafter the House of Cartier sold articles, netting the equivalent of $370,000 in Russia.

111. Fern Spray platinum and diamonds, 7¼ inches in width, Charpentier, Paris 1903. Art of Cartier Collection, Geneva.
This versatile article could be worn as a diadem, a necklace, or an identical pair of brooches. Each element is formed of fifteen graduated pave- and nukkegraub-set diamond double leaves. Entered into the Cartier Paris stock book on November 20, 1903, the fern spray was sold to Sir Ernest Cassel on January 24 of the following year. Sir Ernest was also one of Fabergé's best London clients.

112. Brooch in the Shape of a Tied Ribbon diamond-set platinum with diamonds, 1⁵⁄₁₆ inches wide, engraved Cartier, Paris, 1907. Art of Cartier Collection, Geneva.
Entered into the Paris stock book on February 25, 1907, this brooch displays an early and very modern design with an audacious use of platinum.

113. Seated Bulldog granite with gold and rubies, 2⅝ inches, by Varangoz, Paris, 1907. Art of Cartier Collection, Geneva.
This article was entered into Cartier Paris stock book on November 24, 1907. The bulldog with its gold collar and ruby eyes represents Cartier's response to the hardstone animal figures of Fabergé.

114. Study of a Daisy mother-of-pearl and hardstone, 7 inches in height, apparently unmarked. Private Collection.
In contrast to the floral studies by Fabergé, virtually all of which rely on rock crystal vases to simulate water content, this rival article by Cartier contains the flower in a jasper pot on a square white quartz base set into a glass case on a wooden base.

Frédérick Boucheron and René Lalique

The Frenchman Frédérick Boucheron apprenticed for nine years and worked for another five at his trade before opening his own establishment in Paris in 1866. His oeuvre can be linked to that of Fabergé in a number of ways, both through its great originality and creativity and the highly innovative use of materials of little intrinsic value, such as boxwood, rock crystal, and damascened steel. Boucheron began to prospect the Russian market in 1891, and in 1903 had opened a branch in Moscow located near Fabergé's branch. He started to sell to many of Fabergé's influential clients, including Barbara Kelch, and opened a temporary Russian branch in St. Petersburg on the Nevsky Prospect. The murder of Boucheron's representatives – who had been forewarned of the dangers – on their return from a sales mission to Kiev in 1911, put an end to Boucheron's Russian activities.

René Lalique, undoubtedly the greatest of Fabergé's French competitors for the title 'finest craftsman,' is never mentioned in connection with Fabergé. Born in 1860, he apprenticed as a goldsmith for two years, traveled to England for another two, and returned to Paris where he worked for a time as a designer for Cartier, among others. In 1884, Lalique exhibited his own jewelry designs for the first time and founded his establishment a year later. It was not until a decade later, however, that Lalique publicly exhibited his jewelry for the first time, supplying the great actress, Sarah Bernhardt, with stage jewelry.

His jewels, often crafted of the humblest of materials, reveal highly original and unique designs and superb craftsmanship. These characteristics of Lalique's oeuvre, therefore, provide perfect parallels for those articles created by the House of Fabergé. Unlike Cartier, Lalique never sought to expand his activities beyond the borders of France.

115. Figure of a Japanese Painter silver-gilt, *cloisonné* and *plique-à-jour* enamel, glass base, 12¾ inches, signed Boucheron, 1877. Collection Boucheron, Paris.
This figure is an early and important example of the influence of Oriental art, particularly Japanese, on French designers of the Period.

116. Bonbonnière in the Shape of Two Intersecting Cubes enameled silver-gilt and *cloisonné* enamel, 4⁷⁄₁₆ inches in length, signed Boucheron, 1880. Collection Boucheron, Paris.
This article, lavishly decorated with polychromed *cloisonné* enamels, exhibits a highly original design decorated in Japanese taste that became popular in both Europe and Russia in the 1880s.

117. Episcopal Crozier

enameled, gem-set, silver-gilt, and diamonds 17^3⁄$_4$ inches. Collection Boucheron, Paris.

This ecclesiastical article is justly hailed as one of Boucheron's most celebrated works in the Gothic style. In the shape of a shepherd's staff, the crozier's acanthus scrolls within the crook depict St. Michael the Archangel defeating the Devil. The surround of flowers is decorated with rose-cut diamonds.

118. Belt Buckle in the Shape of a Double Cornucopia

enameled gold, 2^3⁄$_4$ inches in length, signed Boucheron, 1903. Collection Boucheron, Paris. The green horns on this belt buckle are filled with chased gold fruit. Its design may be profitably compared to contemporary articles created by both Cartier and Fabergé.

119. Brooch in the Antique Style gold-mounted diamond-set, 1$\frac{13}{16}$ inches in diameter, signed Boucheron, 1910. Collection Boucheron, Paris.

This circular brooch in the Antique style features a nymph playing a double flute before an altar. Its design is unusually modern and its technique progressive, anticipating trends associated with Art Déco of the 1920s to 1930s. The brooch was formerly in the collection of Elton John.

120. Chalice enameled gold-mounted ivory and glass, 4$\frac{3}{4}$ inches, signed Lalique, 1899-1901. Private Collection, New York.

The cup and foot of this article are decorated with greenish *plique-à-jour* enamel leaves with blackened stems. The cup is additionally set with ivory plaques each carved with three heads, alternating with hexagonal glass cabochons. Its stem contains an ivory frieze of naked figures held by two openwork rings set with cabochons.

121. Pendant diamond-set enameled gold-mounted ivory, 2$\frac{3}{4}$ inches in length, signed Lalique, 18 July 1990. Private Collection, New York.

The Kiss pendant depicts two kissing figures entwined in ivy.

122. Pendant enameled gold, 1$\frac{3}{4}$ inches in length, signed Lalique. Private Collection, New York.

This pendant in the Art Nouveau style depicts an Egyptian woman in profile wearing a wig. Her head is surrounded by large poppy blossoms.

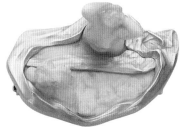

Fabergé and fashion

Although himself not a couturier, Fabergé did influence Russian fashion. A tradition still maintains that ball gowns for the numerous galas of St. Petersburg were not commissioned by socialites until they determined the color of Fabergé's latest enamel, and they insisted upon fabrics to match. However unfounded that tradition may be, the fact remains that articles from the House of Fabergé did accessorize the gowns and suits of the rich and famous. It is perhaps unnecessary to refer to the necklaces, pendants, brooches, bracelets, and cuff links which the firm manufactured and which one takes for granted. The House of Fabergé created a complete line of other accessories as well, such as cane and parasol handles, fans, and lorgnettes and opera glasses. A selection of these articles are on view in this environment together with a selection of ball gowns created by the St. Petersburg couturier August Lazarevich Brisac, whose fashionable shop was extremely popular from the 1890s until the Russian Revolution of 1917.

It is therefore quite easy to lose sight of the fact that Fabergé created his articles not to be placed into museum exhibition showcases but rather to please men and women who actually used many of these creations on a daily basis. In this day and age, when just about anything qualifies as either art or fashion, it is refreshing to encounter articles such as these created by the House of Fabergé, for which quality and technical achievement were matters of the utmost concern in the creation of aesthetically beautiful yet utilitarian objects.

123. Cape Clasp gem-set enameled two-color gold with diamonds, a ruby, and moonstones, 5⅛ inches in length, signed Fabergé with initials of Henrik Wigström, 1899–1908. Private Collection.

The two lateral clasps of triangular shape are decorated with laurel sprays. These clasps are joined by a gold chain which suspends a similarly, but smaller, shaped triangular pendant.

124. Fan jeweled enameled gold, mother-of-pearl, chicken skin, and diamonds, 9 inches in length, signed Fabergé, with initials of Henrik Wigström, 1908–17. The Kremlin Armory Museum. This luxuriously appointed fan features an 18th-century-inspired vignette, painted and signed by van Garden, depicting ladies and gentlemen milling about on a terrace with an extensive landscape beyond.

125. Pair of Lorgnettes gold-mounted and enamel, 4⅜ inches in length, signed by Fabergé, with initials of Henrik Wigström, 1908–17. Private Collection. Fabergé's product line extended to optics as this pair of lorgnettes reveals. It relies for its decorative effect on chased gold laurel and acanthus motifs.

126. Pair of Hairpins diamond-set tortoise shell, 3½ inches in length, unmarked. André Ruzhnikov.

The classic shape and color of these articles are enhanced by the addition of the diamonds.

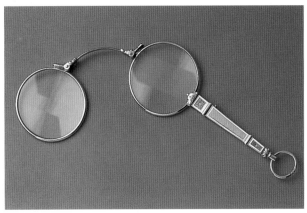

Henrik Wigström and Fabergé's prestigious commissions

Born in southern Finland, the son of a church warden, Henrik Wigström apprenticed at the age of ten to Peter Madsen, a local jeweler who often subcontracted for retail jewelers in St. Petersburg. At the age of 22, Wigström became an assistant to Fabergé's chief workmaster, Michael Perchin. When Perchin died prematurely in 1903, his workshop passed to Wigström, who so distinguished himself that in time this workshop was entrusted with Fabergé's most prestigious and exacting commissions, particularly those created for the Russian imperial family. The sheer profusion of Fabergé Imperial Easter Eggs in this gallery is ample demonstration of his talents. Wigström assisted Perchin with the creation of 26 such masterpieces, and he was responsible for an additional 20.

So valued an employee was Wigström, that he maintained his own shop on the second floor of Fabergé's flagship establishment in St. Petersburg after 1900, and he and his wife Ida were allowed to reside in the same building in separate quarters.

The number of craftsmen in Wigström's workshop diminished drastically with the outbreak of World War I. By 1918, the Russian Revolution had forced the complete closure of the House of Fabergé. The 56 year-old Wigström retreated almost empty-handed to his summer house in Finland, where he died in 1923. Recently friends and former neighbors of the Wigström family, during a routine spring cleaning, discovered a dusty folio volume, unnoticed for over eight decades. This *Wigström Album* contains about 1,000 drawings of articles actually created in his workshop and opens a new window into the career of this extraordinary workmaster. Many of the objects illustrated can be specifically associated with some of Fabergé's most famous clients, who commissioned, purchased from stock, or received as gifts articles which the firm created during the period from 1911 to 1916.

127. The Yusupov Jeton gold and enamel, 1 inch in length, apparently unmarked. Private Collection, courtesy A. von Solodkoff.

The octagonal medallion with a suspension ring is decorated on one side with the crowned initials of Princess Irina Alexandrovna of Russia and the date 9-11-1914. The reverse is similarly decorated with the initials of Prince Felix Yusupov Sumarokov Elston. The two were husband and wife, she being the niece of Tsar Nicholas II and he the mastermind behind the assassination of Rasputin.

128. Art Nouveau Match Holder gold, jasper, demantoids, and rubies, 2⅝ inches, marks: FABERGE, initials of Henrik Wigström. The FORBES Magazine Collection, New York. This octagonal-shaped jasper match holder is decorated with chased gold foliage motifs set with rubies, demantoids, and lions' masks. Its gold base is decorated with alternating leaf-motifs and miniature dolphins whose curled tails support the holder.

129. Nobel Ice Egg platinum, silver, enamel, diamonds, and pearls, 4 inches in length. The FORBES Magazine Collection, New York.

Commissioned by the wealthy Swedish industrialist Dr. Emanuel Nobel, the Nobel Ice Egg is blanketed in layers of transparent and silvery-white translucent enamels through which a partially engraved and finely painted hoarfrost pattern peeks. It was designed by Alma Theresia Pihl, a niece of Albert Holmström, its author. Her subtle design is interrupted solely by a delicate ring of seed pearls, which divides the egg horizontally. When opened, the egg's surprise is a trapezoidal-shaped pendant watch in a fitted velvet-lined compartment with a notch for its chain. The rock-crystal cover of the pendant is decorated with a tracery of platinum-mounted frost motifs set with diamonds. A watch face is visible through a transparent window in the otherwise frosted surface.

Dr. Emanuel Nobel was considered one of Fabergé's most important patrons outside aristocratic circles. The nephew of the inventor Alfred Nobel, Dr Nobel ran the family's highly successful Petroleum Production Company upon the deaths of his father Ludwig in 1888 and his brother Carl in 1898. Under his directorship, the Nobel Diesel engine was introduced. In 1914, about the same time as the Nobel Ice Egg was commissioned, Dr. Nobel moved to Russia where he remained with his family until the 1917 Revolution forced their return to his native Sweden.

130. The Uspensky Cathedral Egg, also known as the Moscow Kremlin Egg gold and enamel, 14¼ inches, signed Fabergé, 1904. The Kremlin Armory Museum.

Presented by Tsar Nicholas II to his wife Tsarina Alexandra Feodorovna on Easter 1906 in commemoration of their 1903 visit to Moscow, the first since their coronation in 1896, this egg cost 11,800 roubles, just under $6,000. The delay between the dates of its creation and presentation was prompted by the Russo-Japanese War.

The egg's subject is the Uspensky Cathedral – the Cathedral of the Assumption – in Moscow's Kremlin. Its enameled gold composition centers on the egg-shaped removable dome, revealing an interior so meticulously crafted that one can actually see the interior's carpets, icons, and high altar. Its pedestal consists of reproductions of Spasskaia and Vodovsvodnaia towers. The clock chimes and a music box, triggered by a key, plays 'Izhe Khveruviny', the Cherubim hymn, a favorite of the Tsar's.

There are interesting symbolic overtones to this, the largest of the surviving Imperial Easter eggs. The prominence given to the ladder of 35 steps is often regarded as symbolic of one's spiritual ascent toward God. On the other hand, the ladder may have Masonic overtones symbolizing the successive paths of enlightenment in the quest for truth.

131. Alexander III Commemorative Egg rock crystal, gold, diamonds, 6⅛ inches, signed Fabergé. The Moscow Kremlin Armory.

Tsar Nicholas II presented this egg to his mother, the dowager empress Maria Feodorovna, on Easter, 1910. Its subject commeorates the 1909 unveiling in Znamensky Square of the controversial, monumental bronze statue of her late husband, Tsar Alexander III, by the sculptor, Prince Pavel Troubetskoy. The price of the egg was 14,700 roubles, the equivalent of $7,350. During the Russian Revolution Troubetskoy's bronze statue was removed from its place of honor and has only recently been relocated in front of the Marble Palace.

132. Fifteenth Anniversary Egg gold, enamel, diamonds, and rock crystal, 5¹/₈ inches, marks: FABERGE, dated, 1894. The FORBES Magazine Collection, New York.

The opalescent and opaque white enamel Fifteenth Anniversary Egg is encased within a grid-shaped cage-work of gold and green enamel garlands which frame 18 superbly painted scenes by court miniaturist Vassily Zuiev. In astonishing detail, the principle events of Tsar Nicholas II and Tsarina Alexandsra's reign over the previous 15 years are chronicled in these historical vignettes. The skill of Zuiev as a miniaturist has often been overlooked in more traditional histories of art. This is unfortunate inasmuch as his historical vignettes on this egg in particular display all the stylistic characteristics of the finest French academic painting of the 19th century. His indebtedness to David and Neo-classicism is very much in evidence, as is shown by comparing his depiction of the coronation of Nicholas II on this egg with David's 'Coronation of Napoleon and Josephine'. But one must always remember that here Zuiev's scene measures barely one square inch whereas David's canvas measures 20x30 feet! Despite the presence of these highly accomplished vignettes of milestone historical events, this egg is perhaps the most personal of all of those presented to the tsarina because intercalated among the historical events are individual portraits not only of herself but also of her husband and five children, each of which is set within oval-shaped apertures bordered by diamonds. The dates of their wedding – 1894 – and of the fifteenth anniversary of their coronation – 1911 – are set beneath the portraits of the tsarina and tsar, respectively. Beneath a table diamond at the top of the egg is the crowned monogram of Tsarina Alexandra; the base is set with a rose-cut diamond.

133. Orange Tree Egg gold, enamel, nephrite, diamonds, citrines, amethysts, rubies, pearls, agate, feathers, with its original silver key, 11³/₄ inches, marks: FABERGE, dated 1911. The FORBES Magazine Collection, New York.

Presented by Tsar Nicholas II to his mother, the dowager empress Maria Feodorovna on Easter 1911, a silver key allowed her to discover the surprise hidden within. Tucked into the finely engraved nephrite leaves, citrine, amethyst, ruby and champagne diamond fruit and white enamel flowers with diamond-set pistils are a winding mechanism and an elliptical button. When triggered by the key in combination, a section of the foliage at the top of the tree rises. Suddenly, music fills the air as a feathered nightingale emerges warbling sweetly while moving its head, wings, and beak. When the melody ends, the bird descends automatically back into its verdant nest until beckoned once more to sing its enchanting tune.

Although there are some connoisseurs who wish to identify the tree as a Bay Leaf, a biographical investigation into the life of Tsarina Maria Feodorovana reveals that the inspiration for this particular egg was doubtless an 18th-century orange tree maintained in a trellised tub in the petit salon in Hyidöre, Denmark. It was here that she passed many pleasant moments in the company of her sister, the widowed queen Alexandra of England.

134. Cross of St. George Egg

silver, gold, enamel, and rock crystal, 3⁵₁₆ inches [without its stand], marks: FABERGE, dated 1916. The FORBES Magazine Collection, New York.

A gesture to wartime austerity because of its simple silver shell, the Cross of St. George Egg presented to dowager empress Maria Feodorovna on Easter 1916 commemorates the 1915 presentation of the Order of St. George Cross to her son, Tsar Nicholas II. Her reaction was heart-felt, as revealed in a letter written shortly after to her son: 'Christ has indeed risen! I kiss you three times and thank you with all my heart for your dear cards and lovely egg with miniatures, which dear old Fabergé brought himself. It is beautiful.'

The Order was originally created by Catherine the Great to be awarded to members of the army, and not to the sovereign, for military bravery. Tsar Nicholas II was presented with the highest class of the Order for his military leadership during World War I. His 12-year-old son Alexei, who had joined him at military headquarters, received a lower grade of the Order. The matte opalescent white enamel egg is under-painted with a green enamel garlanded trellis, which frames St. George crosses in white and red enamel. A ribbbon in the Order's colors of black and orange, encircles two medals; one mounted with the Order of the Cross of St. George, and the second of silver, chased with the portrait of Tsar Nicholas II in profile which indicates that this is the egg's front. When a small button below both medals is pushed, the badges lift to reveal painted miniatures of Tsar Nicholas II and Tsarevich Alexei, respectively. The silver crowned monogram of the dowager empress Maria Feodorovna surmounts the egg; the date of presentation in silver is set directly below.

This egg was the last one created by Fabergé and the last to be personally delivered by Fabergé to the dowager empress Maria Feodorovna before the outbreak of the Russian Revolution. In the year in which she received this egg, she traveled from St. Petersburg to Kiev supervising Red Cross activities in the south before moving to the Crimea. The Bolsheviks searched her residence there but missed her jewelry cases. As a result of their oversight, she was able to take this egg, along with other valuables, when she left the Crimea for England aboard the battleship MSS *Marlborough* in April 1919. The Cross of St. George Egg is therefore the only Imperial Easter Egg created by Fabergé ever to have left Russia with its proper owner.